DIVINATION, **MAGIC,** and HEALING

DIVINATION, **MAGIC**, and HEALING

THE BOOK OF JEWISH FOLKLORE

RONALD H. ISAACS

JASON ARONSON INC.
Northvale, New Jersey
Jerusalem

This book was set in 12 pt. Times Roman by Alabama Book Composition of Deatsville, Alabama.

10   9   8   7   6   5   4   3   2   1

Library of Congress Cataloging-in-Publication Data

Isaacs, Ronald H.
    Divination, magic, and healing : the book of Jewish folklore / by
  Ronald H. Isaacs.
        p.   cm.
    Includes bibliographical references and index.
    ISBN 0–7657–9951–0
    1. Jews—Folklore.   I. Title.
  GR98.I83   1997
  398.2′089924—dc21   97-48

Manufactured in the United States of America. Jason Aronson Inc. offers books and cassettes. For information and catalog write to Jason Aronson Inc., 230 Livingston Street, Northvale, NJ 07647.

Contents

INTRODUCTION

Jewish folklore and the Jewish religion have always influenced each other. Often adapted from foreign sources, Jewish folklore was imbued with the Jewish religious spirit but left its mark on Jewish religion. Although many of the religious practices existing in the various Jewish communities have long ago freed themselves from their superstitious and folkloristic beliefs and bear the character of monotheistic Judaism, there still exists side by side with "normative Judaism" a well of popular beliefs, folklore, and superstitions. Contrary to the explicit command of the Torah that forbids such things as soothsaying and divination, beliefs in divination, the prognostic arts, interpretations of dreams, magic, and astrology are still rooted in many Jewish communities and may even be practiced.

Judged by the popularity of horoscopes, fortune telling, dream interpretation, and magic and the ever-growing number of books on these subjects, many people still believe that these disciplines can and do have an impact on their lives. This volume attempts to contribute to one's understanding of folk Judaism, its beliefs, and practices. It includes chapters on the Jewish calendar and the Jewish signs of the zodiac, the moon and the sun in Jewish folklore, astrology, sorcery and magic, dreams and dream interpretation, superstitions, divination, demonology, the evil eye, and folk remedies for healing. The material presented in this volume is culled from both biblical and rabbinic literature whose works continue to influence Jewish communities throughout the world.

I hope that the readers of this book will have their minds opened to the imaginative and wondrous world of Jewish folklore whose ideas continue to remain widely popular to this day.

Divination, Magic & Healing

Isaacs

J. Aronson

JAAS10

Jewish Calendar—the Measure of Time

IN BIBLE TIMES

Primitive people had no calendar. They only knew of the regular recurrence of the year's cycle from sowing time to harvest time. Observation of the moon's phases eventually led to the knowledge that twelve moon cycles correspond to one cycle of the sun.

Since biblical times, the months and years of the Jewish calendar have been established by the cycles of the moon and the sun. The months are determined by the moon's circuit around the earth. At the same time, they must always be governed by the earth's revolution around the sun.

The Jewish people's attainment of freedom became the beginning point for Israel's historical counting. The Bible, in its account of the liberation from Egypt, says, "This month shall be the beginning of the months, the very first of the month" (Exodus 12:2). The spring season was the beginning of the year, according to the Bible, designating

1

both nature's rebirth and the birth of human freedom. It was also the season of liberation, and as such a logical beginning point for a nation's historical counting. Every calendar day then becomes a reminder of liberation and an appeal to the members of a nation to dedicate themselves ever anew to its ideals. In time, Judaism came to see itself as a world religion. An additional beginning date had to be introduced, with meaning for all, and this was the day of the world's creation.

TEMPLE TIMES

Israel had been given divine authority to sanctify the seasons. The fixation of the month in Temple times was determined on the basis of both calculation and observation. When witnesses appeared before the Supreme Court or the Great Sanhedrin and reported having seen the new moon, they were thoroughly examined on the thirtieth day of the month. If their testimony was found reliable, the day was declared Rosh Chodesh, a new month, and the preceding month had twenty-nine days. If no reliable witnesses appeared, the day was added to the previous month, making it a month of thirty days, and the following day was kept as Rosh Chodesh. The decision of the Sanhedrin was immediately proclaimed in Jerusalem, and messengers were sent out to outlying districts in Israel to announce the day of the new month, so that the festivals coming within the month might be observed by all on the same day. However, because the messengers could not reach Jewish communities outside Judea in time to inform them of the exact day of the new moon, it became customary for the Jews in the Diaspora to observe two festival days instead of one, in order to be certain of observing the proper day.

Rosh Hashanah, the New Year festival, was observed for two days even in Jerusalem, because there it was uncertain as to which was the first day of Tishri, the month of the new year. Yom Kippur, the Day of Atonement, has nowhere been observed for more than one day, because of the hardship of fasting two days in succession. This custom of keeping two festival days in the Diaspora is referred to as *yom tov sheni shel galiyot*—the second festival day in the Diaspora. Even now when all festivals are fixed and calculated with ease ahead of time, it has the force of law hallowed by time, and cannot be abrogated by an individual community of observant Jews.

CALCULATION OF THE YEAR

Originally, the Jewish year had no number of its own. The Bible had no uniform system of dating but employed, for chronology, important historical events such as the exodus from Egypt, an earthquake, or the beginning of a king's reign. During the period of the Second Temple, use was made of the Seleucidan Era, which began in 312 B.C.E. It was called *minyan shetarot* (era of documents), because, perhaps, all documents during the Syrian rule and after had to be dated according to this method in order to be legally valid.

From the Greek conquest of Judea (321 B.C.E.) to the middle of the seventh century, the *minyan shetarot* was in

vogue for all practical purposes. The method of counting
from the traditional date of creation is first mentioned in the
earliest postbiblical chronicle called *Seder Olam Rabbah* of
the second century. Creation was conceived as having
occurred in the fall. Using the genealogy found in the Book
of Genesis, the rabbis added together the life spans of the
early generations and combined them with the time that had
elapsed since then to arrive at the age of the world. This era,
referred to as *anno mundi* (in the year of the world), begins
3760 years before the common era. Thus, the year 5757
since the world's creation corresponds to 1997, the year in
which this book is being written.

THE JEWISH CALENDAR: A BRIEF SUMMARY

As the Sanhedrin was about to be disbanded, a permanent
calendar had to be established to adjust the lunar and solar
year. The adoption of an astronomically fixed calendar,
about the middle of the fourth century, made it possible for
Jews everywhere to determine the first day of the month
without actual observation of the lunar phases. It has been
noted that the Jewish calendar is the most brilliant achieve-
ment of its kind. It was during the administration of
Patriarch Hillel II (330–365) that this amazingly accurate
system of intercalation, equalizing the solar and lunar years,
was published in order to preserve the uniform observance
of the festivals in the face of persecutions, which prevented
Jewish communication with the Babylonian communities.

  There are twelve lunar months in the Jewish calendar.
Each of them has either twenty-nine or thirty days. Because

the lunar year totals 354 days, whereas the solar year amounts to 365-and-a-quarter days, it is necessary to periodically add an extra month in order to reconcile them. Approximately once every three years, a thirteenth month called Adar II is added. A year in which Adar II is intercalated is known as a leap year, of which there are seven in every period of nineteen years.

The names of the months come from Babylonia and Persia, where astronomy flourished. Some of these names are found in the later books of the Bible, such as the Book of Esther.

Each month holds its own message based on the agricultural and historical events that it commemorates. The following are the names of the months of the Jewish year, beginning with the spring. Listed with each month are the festivals that occur in that month:

Nisan is the month of the rebirth of nature. Passover, the festival of liberation, is celebrated on the fourteenth of Nisan, and Holocaust Remembrance Day on the seventeenth.

Iyar is the month of the ripening spring harvest. The fourth of this month is Yom Hazikaron (Remembrance Day), an Israeli memorial day observed for soldiers killed in defense of Israel from the War of Independence (1948) through the present day. On the fifth of Iyar Yom Haazmaut (Israel Independence Day) is celebrated, commemorating the establishment of the State of Israel on May 14, 1948, corresponding to the fifth of Iyar, 5708.

Sivan commemorates the revelation of God to the Israelites atop Mount Sinai. Shavuot, occurring on the sixth of Sivan, commemorates the Israelites' receiving of the

Torah at Mount Sinai. Shavuot, like Passover and Sukkot, is one of the three pilgrimage festivals. During Temple times, Israelites brought an offering of their first fruits, called *bikkurim*, to the Temple in Jerusalem. Yom Yerushalayim (Jerusalem Day) is celebrated on the twenty-eighth of Iyar and commemorates the reunification of the city of Jerusalem.

Tammuz is the month in which a fast day has been proclaimed. In Tammuz, a breach was made in the Jerusalem walls by the Babylonians in the year 586 B.C.E. This happened on the seventeenth of the month, and thus a fast called the Fast of the Seventeenth of Tammuz is observed by traditional Jews.

Av is the month of deepest mourning. On the ninth of this month both the first and second Temples went up in flames. A fast day called Tisha b'Av (ninth of Av) commemorates this day of mourning and sadness.

Elul is the month of preparation for the so-called Days of Awe. Each day (with the exception of the Sabbath) includes the sounding of the ancient ram's horn, called the *shofar*, awakening the Jewish people to begin to look introspectively and repent for their mistakes and transgressions.

Tishri calls upon the Jewish people to begin anew, starting a new year by acknowledging God as Sovereign and Judge of the world. This is the message of Rosh Hashanah (the New Year), which begins on the first of this month. The fast of Yom Kippur (Day of Atonement) falls on the tenth of this month. On this day Jews confess their shortcomings and pledge to renew their spirits and souls. On the fourteenth of the month the holiday of

Sukkot (booths) is observed. Jews offer thanks to God for the fall harvest and shelter, pledging to sanctify the gifts of nature by using them to the benefit of humankind. Finally, before returning to one's daily routine, Jews embrace the Torah, celebrating Shemini Atzeret on the twenty-second of Tishri and Simchat Torah on the twenty-third.

The month of Cheshvan, sometimes known as Marcheshvan, is unique in that no Jewish holidays are celebrated in this month.

Kislev is the month in which the Festival of Lights, Hanukkah, is celebrated. On the twenty-fifth of this month, the Jewish people place the lights of Hanukkah at their windows, visible to the world and reminding all of the miracle of freedom.

Tevet is the month that marks the beginning of the siege of Jerusalem by the Babylonians, which began on the tenth day of the month.

Shevat, tree-planting time in Israel, reminds the Jewish people of their bond with the land. On the fifteenth of the month the New Year's Day of Trees, called Tu b'Shvat, is celebrated.

Adar is the month that brings us the Fast of Esther on the thirteenth, and Purim, the Festival of Lots, on the fourteenth. This holiday commemorates a miraculous escape from persecution by the Jews of Persia, who through the intervention of Mordecai's niece Queen Esther, the Jews were saved.

The Sun and the Moon in Jewish Tradition

THE MOON IN BIBLICAL AND RABBINIC WRITINGS

In the narrative of the story of the Creation, the moon is indicated, without any special name, as one of the two great luminaries. Relative to the sun, it was described as "the lesser light to rule the night" (Genesis 1:16). In the Book of Psalms 104:19, it is expressly stated that the moon was created in order to indicate the seasons.

Like other celestial bodies, the moon was believed to have an influence on the universe as a whole. Its injurious influence on humans is referred to in Psalm 121:6, where it is told that the moon will not strike by night. It was also believed that the moon caused epilepsy.

Because the moon was regarded by many Oriental nations as a divinity, its worship was expressly forbidden to the Israelites, as can be attested to by the prohibition mentioned in the Book of Deuteronomy (17:3). The Israelites were known to have practiced for many years the cult of the "Queen of Heaven," a likely reference to moon worship.

A sign of God's anger was often portrayed as a lunar eclipse in the Bible. The Book of Isaiah 13:10–11 refers to a moon that shall diffuse no glow as a sign of evil in the world. Restoration of moonlight, and sunlight too, was a sign in the Book of Isaiah (3:26) that God will have restored the Israelites to their former state.

Several interesting rabbinic legends relate to the moon and its designation in the Bible as "the lesser light." In one, Rabbi Simeon ben Pazzi declared that at the time of the creation of the world the moon was the same size as the sun. The moon proceeded to object that it would not be appropriate for two kings to use one crown. It was then that God decided that it would be best to diminish the size of the moon, offering to her as a compromise the fact that the Jewish people would heretofore count the years using the phases of the moon. In addition, God consoled the moon by stating that in the future certain righteous people would also bear the moon's epithet, namely that of "the smaller one" (e.g., Jacob in Amos 7:5 and David in I Samuel 17:14). This was not enough assurance to the moon who, according to the Talmudic tradition, continued to remain discontented. It was then that God required that a he-goat be sacrificed on the first of every month as a sin offering for His having the moon's size diminished (Talmudic *Chullin* 60b).

In a second midrash God appeased the complaints of the moon by surrounding her with a host of stars, thus turning her into a queen (Genesis Rabbah 6, 3–4).

According to the Talmud (*Sukkah* 29a), an eclipse of the moon is considered a bad sign for the Jews. The eclipse of the moon is caused by four kinds of transgressions: forgery, false witness, breeding small cattle in Palestine, and cutting down fruit trees.

According to another midrash, the reason why the Jewish people count the days of the year by the moon is that just as the moon reigns both at night and during the day, so too the Jewish people possess both this world and the world-to-come (Genesis Rabbah 6:2).

In one rabbinic tradition the moon was designated as Jacob's luminary, while the sun symbolized Esau (Genesis Rabbah 6:3). The rabbis declared that the countenance of Joshua was like that of the sun (Talmud *Bava Batra* 75a). Queen Esther, who brought light to Israel after the evil decree of King Ahasueras, is likewise compared to the moon, which enables people to walk about when it lights up the darkness of the night (Exodus Rabbah 15:6).

SANCTIFICATION OF THE MOON

The moon, because of its monthly reappearance, is often considered as the emblem of Israel. Israel, like the moon, has undergone phases of persecution throughout its history, always emerging anew without being destroyed. Also, like the moon, the Jewish people regularly reappear after being temporarily eclipsed. It is for this reason that a ceremony for the sanctification of the new moon, known as *kiddush levanah*, was created during Talmudic times.

The new-moon blessing is customarily recited in the open air when the moon is visible between the fourth and the sixteenth of the month, preferably on a Saturday night, after *Havdalah*, when the traditional Jew is in a joyous frame of mind.

The four synonyms referring to the Creator in one of the passages of the blessing have as their initials the letters that spell the name *ya'akov* (Jacob), alluding to his descendants, the people of Israel. The passage reads: *"baruch yotzrecha . . . osecha . . . konecha, borecha."*

The expression "Long live David, King of Israel" refers to Psalm 89:38, which says that David's dynasty shall "like the moon be established forever." The numerical value of this line in Hebrew *"David melech yisrael chai ve-kayam"* (819) is equal to that of Rosh Chodesh, the new month. Interestingly, it became the password of Bar Kochba's army.

The blessing of the new moon opens with a benediction praising the Creator of the celestial lights who ordained the monthly renewal of the moon. In the Talmudic tractate of *Sofrim* (20:1–2) several mystifying details are prescribed in connection with the blessing. They are as follows: The blessing of the moon must take place at the end of the Sabbath when one is in a jovial mood and dressed in pleasant garments. The worshiper is expected to look directly at the moon, stand straight and erect with feet together, and recite the benediction. The worshiper should say three times *"siman tov"*—a good sign—and perform three dancing gestures in the direction of the moon while saying three times: Just as I cannot touch you, may my enemies never be able to harm me. Then the worshiper should say *"shalom"*—peace—to his neighbor three times and go home with a happy heart.

The basic text of the new-moon blessing is presented in the Talmudic tractates of *Sanhedrin* (42a) and *Soferim* (2:1). Many additions since that time have subsequently been made. In the present Ashkenazi ritual, the blessing is usually introduced by the recital of Psalms 148:1–6 (in the Sephardic rite also Psalm 8:4–5) after which the blessing praising God as the Sovereign One over nature is pronounced. Here is the text of the new moon blessing:

Rabbi Yochanan: Whoever blesses the new moon at the proper time is considered as having welcomed the presence of the *Shechinah*.

Halleluyah. Praise God from the heavens. Praise God, angels on high. Praise God, sun and moon and all shining stars. Praise God, highest heavens. Let them praise the glory of God at whose command they were created, at whose command they endure forever and by whose laws nature abides (Psalm 148:1–6) (Ashkenazic ritual).

When I behold Your heavens, the work of Your fingers, the moon and stars that You set into place. What is man that You have been mindful of him, mortal man that You have taken note of him.

Praised are You, Adonai our God, Sovereign of the Universe whose word created the heavens, whose breath created all that they contain. Statutes and seasons God set for them, that they should not deviate from their given task. Gladly, they do the will of their Creator, whose work is dependable. To the moon God spoke: renew yourself, crown of glory for those who were borne in the womb, who also are destined to be renewed and to extol their Creator for His glorious sovereignty. Praised are You, God, who renews the months.

David, King of Israel, lives and endures.

Shalom Aleichem. May good fortune be ours, and blessing for the entire household of Israel.

ROSH CHODESH: THE NEW MOON FESTIVAL

Jewish tradition treats the coming of every lunar month with great distinction. On the Sabbath before the festival of the New Moon, called Rosh Chodesh, the day of the new month is announced with much fanfare during the Torah service, and the congregation asks God to make the new month one of life, blessing, and joy. The only exception to the sounding of the shofar on the Sabbath before a new month is that of the month of Tishri, on which Rosh Hashanah occurs. Here Jewish folklore and custom have mandated that the shofar not be sounded on the Sabbath before the new Jewish year, in order to "fool" the Angel of Death. (The Angel of Death traditionally enjoyed playing havoc with people's lives at transitional moments such as that of a new year.)

Some traditional Jews treat the day before the new Jewish month as a small Yom Kippur, when they fast and turn away from their misdeeds of the previous month. This interesting custom arose among the mystics of the holy city of Safed in northern Israel, who in the sixteenth century saw the waning of the moon as a symbol of the exile of God's Presence in the world and of the fragmented state of human existence. For them the new month was a symbol of renewal and hope.

In biblical times, Rosh Chodesh was a minor festival in the life of the Israelites. On this day, special sacrificial offerings were made in honor of the proclamation of the new month and the shofar, the ram's horn, was sounded.

In ancient times, as previously mentioned, the day of the new month was determined by the rabbinic court, based on reports by witnesses who had observed the new moon. Today, by astronomical calculation, the beginning of the new Jewish month takes place at the moment when the moon is exactly between the earth and the sun, and thus nothing is visible of the moon. It is then that the *molad*, or birth of the moon, takes place.

THE SUN IN THE BIBLE

In the times of the Bible, the sun grew to be a deity in a variety of ancient cultures. The Hittites worshiped both a god and goddess of the sun. The sun was worshipped at the temple of Ebabbar in Sippar, in northern Babylonia. The cult of the sun, incredibly popular in Palestine, can be attested to by place names such as Beth-Shemmesh (House of the Sun) or Ir Shemesh (City of the Sun). Deuteronomy 4:19 specifically warns against the worship of the sun: "When you look up at the sky and behold the sun and the moon and the stars . . . you must not be lured into bowing down to them or serving them." It was, nevertheless, introduced into Judah by King Manasseh (II Kings 21:3, 5) who had erected altars in honor of the heavenly hosts.

For the biblical Israelites, the sun was created as "the greater light to rule the day" (Genesis 1:16). Both the sun and the moon appear in Joseph's dream as personifying his parents (Genesis 37:9–10). The sun is shown to be benevolent in II Samuel 23:4 as it is described bringing forth vegetation from the earth. In Ecclesiastes 11:7 the sun is described as sweet light, a delight for the eyes to behold the sun. At times the sun produces evil with its ability to sear and scorch, as described in Psalm 121:6.

The sun has also been used in the Bible (Psalm 72:17) as

a simile of lasting fame. The enduring nature of King David's dynasty is expressed by the statement that his throne shall be before God as the sun. The sun is also portrayed as a symbol of victory and might. In Psalm 84:12 God Himself is described as a sun and a shield. The sun is also portrayed (Malachi 3:20) metaphorically as bearing wings on which, as the sun of righteousness, shall carry healing. The sun has been described as an emblem of beauty in the Song of Songs 6:11 in addition to typifying the progress of a good person toward perfection in Proverbs 4:18.

In the many prophetic apocalyptic descriptions of the end of time, the darkening of the sun at rising is emphasized as one of the signs of impending judgment (Isaiah 13:10). However, in the Day of the Lord, the day on which God will finally defeat all of His enemies and judge all the wicked of Israel for their evil days, Israel will be created anew, while paganism will end. In addition, we are told in the Book of Isaiah (30:26) that the sun will shine seven times more brightly than usual. Additionally, the Book of Isaiah reports that the Israelites will no longer need the sun or the moon, because God's light will be an everlasting one.

The Bible records two interesting miracles of the sun in which the sun itself appears to be suspended in time. In the first wondrous act of the sun (Joshua 10:12–14), Joshua speaks to God when God delivered up the Amorites before the children of Israel. He says, "'Sun, stand still upon Gibeon, and you, moon, in the valley of Aijalon.' And the sun stood still, and the moon stayed until the nation had avenged themselves of their enemies." The ancient rabbis list this passage (*Mechilta, Beshallach*) as one of the occasions when Israel uttered song to God. Some modern commentators attempt to eliminate the supernatural element from the incident by stressing the poetic form of the language, which they understand as implying no more than "may God grant us victory before the sun sets." Other explanations, more scientifically oriented, attempt to deal with the miraculous phenomenon of the sun by describing the possibility of an intense cold in the region of ancient Syria producing a terrible hailstorm, causing the refraction of the sun. Travelers in polar regions give many instances when the sun is seen for several days, when they know the orb is one degree below in the horizon. This refraction is fairly common, and so the explanation goes, it appeared as if the sun has stood still. The Bible assumed that when the sun stops the moon will also stop, and that when the sun goes on the moon will also go on.

In a most interesting text in the Second Book of Kings 20:8–11, King Hezekiah turns ill and asks Isaiah what the sign will be for God to heal him. Here is the continuation of this text:

> And Isaiah said: This shall be the sign for you from God, that God will do the thing that He has spoken: shall the shadow go forward ten degrees, or go back ten degrees. . . . And Isaiah the prophet cried to God and he brought the shadow ten degrees backward . . .

Here we see that the sign of Hezekiah's recuperation will be the retrogression of the sun's shadow as seen on a sun dial. Some commentators have suggested that this incident is based on a solar eclipse or that the movement of the sun's shadow was purely an optical illusion.

THE SUN IN RABBINIC WRITINGS

According to Pirke de Rabbi Eliezer 8, the sun and the moon were both created on the twenty-eighth day of Elul. Originally they were of equal size and strength, but soon jealousy grew between them, as each vied for attention. The moon's size was thus diminished because it had intruded into the domain of the sun.

Rabbi Levi reported in the legendary tale appearing in Genesis Rabbah 6:3 that Esau (i.e., Rome) counted time by the sun, which is large, while Jacob (i.e., Israel) by the moon, which is small. Whereas Esau's sun indicated that he had a share in the world alone, but no portion in the world to come, Jacob, counting by the moon, which ruled both day and night, would have portions both in this world as well as in the world to come.

According to the Midrash (Psalms 19:13), God placed the sun in the second firmament because if He had placed it in the one nearest the earth, which is visible to terrestrial eyes, all would be devoured by its heat. The sun was often described rabbinically as being in a type of cover or bag. According to the Talmud *Nedarim* 8b, the sun in the future would be released from its protective cover and the wicked will be consumed by its incredible heat. In addition, the sun's healing powers will cure all righteous persons of their illnesses.

According to Pirke de Rabbi Eliezer 6 the sun ascends by means of 366 steps and descends by 183 in the east and 183 in the west. There are 366 windows in the firmament, through which the sun successively emerges and withdraws.

The sun is always obeisant to God, bowing down before the Commander. Three letters of God's name are written on the sun's heart and angels lead it—one set by day and one by night. The sun is also described as riding in a chariot. Its face is metaphorically connected to conditions of weather. For example, when looking downward its face and horns are of fire, while when turned upward, of hail.

According to rabbinic tradition, the sun would often be influenced by that which went on in the human realm. For instance, we are told in the Talmud *Nedarim* 39b that the sun and the moon would not rise when Korach was disputing with Moses. In addition, the sun and moon would not agree to give their light to earth until they were assured that justice would be done to the son of Amram (Talmud *Sanhedrin* 110a).

The rabbis differed as to the color of the sun. Rabbi Papa is quoted as saying that the sun is dark red in color at sunrise, because it passes by the roses of the Garden of Eden. Yet the sun is said to appear white during the day on account of the dazzle of its rays on one's eyes (Talmud *Bava Batra* 84a). The Talmud (*Yoma* 28b) states that the humidity of the sun is worse than its heat, and the dazzling and piercing sunlight as it flashes through the clouds is harder to bear than the uncovered sun.

The Talmud deduces the healing effects of sunlight from the biblical verse "But unto you . . . shall the sun of righteousness arise with healing in its wings" (Malachi 3:20; Talmud *Nedarim* 8b). The Talmud (*Bava Batra* 16b) reports that Abraham was in possession of a precious stone that had the capability of healing the sick. When Abraham died, God set the stone in the sphere of the sun.

SIGNS, SYMBOLS, AND OMENS OF THE SUN

According to the Talmud (*Sukkah* 29a), an eclipse of the sun is an evil sign for gentiles. When the solar eclipse occurs in the eastern horizon it forecasts bad tidings for the inhabitants of the East, whereas if it is in the western horizon it is a bad omen for those inhabitants. If it occurs in the zenith it threatens the entire world. When the solar eclipse is red, it is a symbol of war. When the eclipse is gray it is a symbol of famine, and when the sun changes from red to gray, it is a symbol of both war and famine. When the eclipse occurs early in the day or night it forecasts the advent of evil, whereas if it occurs late in the day or night, it is a sign that evil will occur gradually.

The sun is employed as a symbol in the Kabbalistic mystic tradition. Generally, the sun is masculine and represents the principal or independent one. Abraham is the sun, as well as Samuel, because he was independent and accepted no gifts from any persons. The moon, on the other hand, is a symbol of femininity in mystical tradition, representing the secondary dependent one—the mother. Thus Moses and Aaron, the rich and poor person, the Torah and the Talmud, are representative of the sun and the moon, respectively.

According to the Talmud (*Shabbat* 156a), each one of the seven planets predominates during one particular hour of each day and night, exercising a substantial influence on the person both in that particular hour. The one born during the hour of the sun's rising will be of fair complexion, independent, and forthright. The planet Mercury was considered the secretary of the sun, and as a consequence one born during its hour will be bright and most intelligent.

THE SOLAR CYCLE: THE BLESSING OF THE SUN

The solar cycle (called in Hebrew a *machzor*) was a period of twenty-eight years. It was taught by the ancient rabbis (Talmud *Berachot* 59b) that a person who sees the sun at its turning point, the moon in its power, the planets in their orbits, or the signs of the zodiac in their order should say "Praised are You, who makes the work of creation." According to Abaye the sage, this occurs every twenty-eight years, when the cycle begins again and the spring equinox falls in Saturn on the evening of Tuesday, going into Wednesday. This calculation is based on the calendar of Samuel Yarchina'ah, which ascribes to the solar year 365 and one quarter days, and asserts that each of the seven planets rules over one hour of the day in the following sequence: Saturn, Jupiter, Mars, the sun, Venus, Mercury, and the moon. Thus the first planet, Saturn, is seven and one half hours advanced at the beginning of the summer solstice, and thirty hours (one and one quarter days) at the turn of the year, or five days in four years, at the end of which this planet again takes it place at the beginning of the eve of the vernal equinox (Nisan). This period is called in Hebrew the *machzor katan*, or short cycle. A space of five days follows every such cycle, so that the second cycle begins on Monday, the third on Saturday, the fourth on Thursday, the fifth on Tuesday, the sixth on Sunday, and the seventh on Friday. Seven short cycles completes the *machzor gadol* or long cycle of twenty-eight years, then Saturn returns to its original position at the first hour of Wednesday eve and a new solar cycle begins. The modern present solar cycle commenced on the fifth of the Hebrew month of Nisan, in the Jewish year 5657, corresponding to April 7, 1897.

The ceremony of the blessing of the sun is a prayer service in which the sun is blessed in thanksgiving for its creation and its being set into motion in the firmament on the fourth day of creation. The ceremony takes place once every twenty-eight years after the morning service, when the sun is about ninety degrees above the eastern horizon, on the first Wednesday of the month of Nisan (late March–early April). In the twentieth century the blessing occurred on April 1, 1925, March 18, 1953, and April 8, 1981. It will next occur on April 7, 2009.

The blessing customarily begins with verses from the following biblical texts: Psalms 84:12, 72:5, Malachi 3:20, Psalm 97:6, and Psalm 148. The actual blessing is as follows:

> *Baruch ata Adonai elohaynu melech ha'olam oseh ma'asey v'resheet.*
>
> Praised are You, Adonai our God, Sovereign of the Universe, Source of creation.

Following Psalms 19 and 121, the hymn *El Adon* is recited. The ritual generally continues with the following prayer of thanksgiving in which the community expresses thanksgiving for having been sustained and the hope to live and reach the days of the Messiah:

> May it please You, Adonai our God and God of our ancestors, as You have given us life and sustenance and

have permitted us to reach and celebrate this event, so may You lengthen our life and sustenance and make us again worthy to render the blessing on the return of this cycle, which may reach us in gladness in the sight of Your city rebuilt and in the enjoyment of Your service. May we be privileged to see the face of Your Messiah and that the prophecy may be fulfilled.

The ritual ends with the chanting of the *Aleynu* and the Mourner's Kaddish.

NOTABLE QUOTATIONS
RELATED TO THE SUN AND MOON

The following are some of the more interesting passages as culled from rabbinic sources that further illuminate the role of the sun and moon in Jewish folklore. They relate to the light and color of both sun and moon, their mode of travel in the sky, and the omens of an eclipse.

1. We have been taught, and Rabbi said: The moon's column of light is not similar to that of the sun's column of light. Whereas the moon's column of light rises straight like a rod, the sun's column of rays branches out in all directions. (Talmud *Yoma* 28b)

2. Rav said: When the orb of the sun and that of the moon enter to get permission from the Holy One, their eyes become diminished by the radiance of the Presence, so that when they wish to go out to give light to the world, they can see nothing at all. What then does the Holy One do to them? God shoots ahead of them arrows by whose light they go: "When the sun and the moon have come to a standstill in their habitations, they go by the light of Your arrows, by the shining of Your shining spear."

Rabbi Levi said: Each and every day the Holy One has to sit in judgment over the sun and the moon, because the sun and the moon do not wish to go forth to give light to the world. What is the reason? They say, "Mortals offer incense to us, mortals bow down to us." What does the Holy One do about them? Rabbi Yusta bar Shunem said: God sits in judgment over them, until reluctantly they go forth to give light to the world, as is said, "Every morning does God send his judgment to the light, that it does not fail." [*Zephania* 3:5] (Leviticus Rabbah 31:9)

3. When the sun and moon are about to go back in, they are unable to tell where to go because of the radiance from above, and so they stand in the firmament and procrastinate before entering. However, the Holy One hurls torches, arrows, and spears of light before them. And toward the place where God hurls them, there they go. [Psalms 19:11] (Midrash)

4. "The chariot of it is purple" (Song of Songs 3:10). The sun which is set on high, rises in a chariot, and gives light to the world as it rides forth bedecked like a bridegroom, in keeping with the verse "the sun is as a bridegroom coming out of its chamber." [Psalm 19:6] (Numbers Rabbah 12:4)

5. The sun's orb is kept within a sheath, in front of which there is a pool of water. When the sun comes out, the Holy

One tempers its strength in the water, so that as it goes forth it will not incinerate the world. (Genesis Rabbah 6:6)

6. Rabbi Levi said: Why is a person's voice not as audible during the day as it is by night? Because of the orb of the sun, which saws its way through the firmament as a carpenter saws through cedars. (Talmud *Yoma* 20b)

7. Our masters taught: Were it not for the sound made by the sun's orb, the sound of Rome's tumult would be heard. And were it not for the sound of Rome's tumult, the sound of the sun's orb would be heard. (Talmud *Yoma* 20b)

8. Our rabbis taught: The one who sees the sun at its cycle's beginning, the moon in its power, the stars in their orbits and the signs of the zodiac in their original order should say, "Blessed be God who wrought the work of creation." (Talmud *Berachot* 59b)

9. Rabbi Simeon ben Yochai said: We do not know whether the sun and the moon fly through the air, glide across the firmament, or have a regular route assigned to them. It is an exceedingly difficult matter, and no person can comprehend it. (Genesis Rabbah 6:8)

10. The Holy One created three hundred and sixty-five windows for the world to use: one hundred and eighty-two in the east, one hundred and eighty-two in the west, and one in the firmament's middle, out of which the sun issued at the beginning of the work of creation. (Jerusalem Talmud, *Rosh Hashanah* 2:5)

11. Antoninus asked Rabbi, "Why does the sun rise in the east and set in the west?" Rabbi: "Were it the other way

around, you would have asked the very same question."
Antoninus: "My question still stands—why should the sun
set in the west?" Rabbi: "The sun sets in the west to be
obedient to its Maker, as it is written: 'The host of the
heavens prostrate themselves before You'" [Nehemiah 9:6].
Antoninus: "Then let the sun go midway in heaven, prostrate itself, and set immediately." Rabbi: "The sun sinks
gradually for the sake of workers and wayfarers." (Talmud
Sanhedrin 91a)

12. The Israelite sages maintain that the sun travels
beneath the sky by day and above the sky at night. The sages
of the world maintain that the sun travels beneath the sky by
day and below the earth at night. Their view (i.e., sages of
the nations) is preferable to ours, for springs are cold during
the day but not during the night.

We have been taught that Rabbi Nathan said: In the
summer, the sun travels in the high part of heaven, therefore
the entire world is hot, while the springs are cold. In winter,
the sun travels in the lower part of heaven, therefore the
entire world is cold, while the springs are hot.

Our masters instructed: The sun travels over four courses:
during Nisan, Iyar, and Sivan, it travels over the mountains,
in order to melt the snows; during Tammuz, Av and Elul,
over the inhabited world, to ripen the fruits; during Tishri,
Marcheshvan and Kislev, over seas, to dry up the rivers;
during Tevet, Shevat and Adar, through the wilderness, so as
not to dry up the seeds. (Talmud *Pesachim* 95b)

13. Rabbi Judah bar Ilai said: The sun is kept within its
sheath, as is said, "As for the sun, God set into a tent"
[Psalm 19:5]. But during the Tammuz solstice, the sun

emerges from its sheath in order to ripen fruits. (*Tanchuma, Tetzaveh* 6)

14. Rabbi Eliezer the Elder said: By the time the fifteenth day in the month of Av comes, the power of the sun is depleted. (Talmud *Bava Batra* 121b)

15. Our rabbis taught: When the sun is in eclipse, it is a bad omen for the entire world. By what parable can this be compared? By the one of a king of flesh and blood who made a banquet for his servants and put up a banquet for his servants and put up a lamp for them. But when he became angry at them, he said to his attendant, "Take away the lamp from them, and let them sit in the dark."

Our masters taught: When the sun is in eclipse, it is a bad omen for the nations of the world. When the moon is in eclipse, it is a bad omen for Israel, since Israel counts time by the moon, while the nations of the world count it by the sun. If the sun is in eclipse in the east, it is a bad omen for the dwellers in the east. If the sun is in the center of the heaven, it is a bad omen for the entire world. If the sun's appearance is as red as blood, it is a sign that the sword is coming to the world. If it is the color of sackcloth, the arrows of famine are coming to the world. If it resembles both, then both the sword and the arrows of famine are coming to the world.

If the eclipse is at sunset, punishment will be slow in coming. If the eclipse occurs at dawn, punishment will hasten to come to the world. Some others say that the meaning of the signs is reversed.

16. Rabbi Simeon ben Pazzi pointed out a contradiction between the two parts of the verse. The verse begins by saying, "And God made the two great lights" [Genesis 1:16] and then goes on to speak of a "great light" and a "lesser light." This is what happened. The moon dared to the Holy One saying, "Sovereign of the Universe, is it possible for two kings to wear the same size crown?" The Holy One answered, "Go, then, and make yourself smaller." But the moon protested, "Sovereign of the Universe, must I make myself smaller merely because I suggested to You something that is sensible?" The Holy One conceded, "Very well. Go and rule by day as well as night." (Talmud *Chullin* 60b)

17. When the Holy One rebuked the moon, and it fell, some sparks fell from it into the sky—these are the stars. (*Yalkut Reuveni*)

Astronomy

IN THE BIBLE

Astronomy refers to the scientific study of outer space, such as the positions and dimensions and evolution of the stars and planets. Although the Bible contains little in the way of explicit mention of the science of astronomy, there are references to the sky, the sun and moon, stars, and even the planets. This section concentrates on the stars, planets, and the fixed stars.

It is quite clear from the Bible, especially in the Book of Deuteronomy 4:19, that there was always the possibility of the Israelites being lured into bowing down to the celestial bodies. As a precaution against such idolatry, the Bible forbade celestial worship, something that was more common among the Babylonians and Egyptians.

The creation story in the Book of Genesis 1:16 refers to the creation of the lights in the sky, the sun to dominate the day and the moon to dominate the night and the stars. The stars of the heaven are described in Genesis 22:17 as numerous as the sands of the seashore. The stars are often portrayed as living creatures in the Bible. For instance, in the Book of Judges 5:20, the stars themselves are described as fighting against Sisera, the Canaanite king. Rabbinic interpretation has declared the stars to represent the unpaid fighters whom God enlisted to overcome the unpaid hirelings in the Canaanite army. Other more scientific interpretations understood the passage to refer to the stars ruling the seasons and weather, and in this case helping the Israelites against Sisera by flooding the Kishon brook at a critical moment of the battle.

The stars are often biblically described as "the hosts of heaven," acting in a sense as soldiers who serve God. This starry army belonged to God, and thus the frequent expression *Adonai Tzevaot*—the Lord of Hosts (Isaiah 6:3–4), indicating that God was the actual leader of the celestial array. At the head of this starry host stands a captain of the army (Daniel 8:11). According to the passage in Daniel, this captain was the star who was the highest in altitude as well. (Some commentators believed this referred to the planet Saturn, the farthest removed from earth and the highest in the heavens.) In the Book of Chronicles II, 18:18, the stars stand in the Presence of God, to the right and to the left of God's throne.

Several fixed stars are mentioned in biblical passages. For instance, the Hebrew word *kesil* (appearing in Isaiah 13:10, Amos 5:8, Job 9:9, and Job 38:31) has been variously interpreted to mean constellation of stars or more specifically Orion, the constellation in the celestial equator near Gemini and Taurus. The Hebrew word *kimah* appearing in the Book of Amos (5:8) has been understood by some to mean Pleiades, an open star cluster in the constellation Taurus. Other interpretations for *kimah* have included Aldebaran, a bright double star in the constellation Taurus; Arcturus, the fourth brightest star in the sky and the brightest in the constellation Bootes; and Sirius, a star in the constellation Canis Major, the brightest star in the sky. The Hebrew word *mazzarot*, appearing in the Book of Job 9:9 and 38:32, has been interpreted in various ways, including as a reference to Pleiades or Hyades, another cluster of stars in the Taurus constellation.

Finally, "ash" or "ayish" appearing in the Book of Job 9:9 and 38:32, has been interpreted as the Great Bear, a constellation in the region of the north celestial pole near Draco and Leo containing the seven stars that form the Big Dipper.

The planets (in Hebrew *mazzalot* in II Kings 23:5) are, according to some biblical interpreters, in the twelve regions of the firmament, which are later referred to as the signs of the Zodiac. Of the planets, as far as is ascertainable with any degree of certainty, two are mentioned in the Bible. It is generally agreed that *kiyun* (Amos 5:26) refers to Saturn whereas others have interpreted the reference to *milechet hashamayim*—queen of heaven as referring to Venus (Isaiah 7:18). That the latter means Venus has been demonstrated by the cakes that are said to have been baked for her. In addition, among the Assyro-Babylonians the cake offerings were called "the bread of Ishtar" (Venus). Other hypotheses for the ascertaining of planets mentioned in the Bible included the supposition that *gad* in Isaiah 65:11 means Jupiter, the god of fortune and that *meni* in the same verse means Venus.

ASTRONOMY IN THE TALMUD

The Talmudic sages viewed astronomy as an important adjunct to the study of the Torah itself, which was of course considered the highest form of study. Whereas the star-world was to the pagan an object of worship, the Jewish people generally believed that the stars and their alignment determined the destiny of people. There are numerous references to astronomy and its use in the Talmud. This section attempts to summarize a cross-section of those references.

In a remarkable statement in the Talmudic tractate of *Shabbat* 75a, we are informed that it was considered an obligation for a person with great talent to study the science of astronomy. In this passage, Rabbi Simeon ben Pazzi is quoted in the name of Rabbi Joshua ben Levi as saying that the person who knows how to calculate the cycles and planetary courses, and does not, of him the Bible says, "but they regard not the work of God, neither have they considered the operation of his hands." Many rabbinic teachers were skilled in astronomical science, including Rabbi Yochanan ben Zakkai (Talmud *Sukkah* 28a), Rabbi Gamaliel II, and Rabbi Joshua ben Hananiah. According to the Talmudic tractate of *Horayot* (10a), Rabbi Joshua ben Hananiah knew of the existence of a comet that appeared once every seventy years and led mariners astray. It is entirely possible that he was referring to Halley's Comet. In the Ethics of the Fathers (3:18) Rabbi Eleazar ben Chisma declared that astronomy and geometry are the desserts of wisdom.

Among the Babylonian rabbinic scholars, Samuel was important in the astronomical field, claiming in the Talmudic tractate of *Rosh Hashanah* 20b that he was able to calculate and adjust the festival calendar of the Diaspora without the necessity of the more usual eyewitness reports of the new moon in Israel.

The first generations of rabbinic teachers were acquainted with a *beraita* (i.e., a rabbinic source that is not a part of the Mishneh) called "Secrets of Intercalation" in which were written the various precepts for the sanctification and intercalation of the month.

There is a vast array of different opinions regarding conceptions of heaven and earth in rabbinic tradition. In the opinion of some of the rabbinic sages, the earth was considered the center of creation with heaven as a hemisphere spread over it. According to the Talmudic tractate of *Tamid* 32a, the heaven and earth kiss each other at the horizon, and the earth's diameter from east to west is equivalent to the height of the heavens above the earth. The earth rests upon water and is encompassed by it. According to other conceptions, the earth is supported by one, seven, or twelve pillars. These rest upon the water, the water upon the mountains, the mountains upon the wind, and the wind upon the storm (Talmud *Chagigah* 12b).

The ancient nations often believed that the earth was a disk floating atop water. In the Jerusalem Talmud, *Avodah Zarah* 3:42c, it is reported that when Alexander the Great tried to ascend to heaven he rose even higher and higher, until the earth appeared as a globe and the sea as a tray.

Rabbinic opinion held to the belief that the earth as they knew it was preceded by many other worlds that were in some way flawed in the eyes of God and ultimately destroyed. Rabbi Abbahua reports in Genesis Rabbah 3:7 that God went on creating worlds and destroying them until He created this present one and declared "This one pleases me, and those did not please Me." The Midrash of the Book of Psalms 24 reports that God traverses in all eighteen thousand worlds and for this reason is frequently termed "Lord of the Worlds."

According to the kabbalists who were masterminds of the Jewish mystic tradition, there are seven heavens. They are portrayed in the Talmudic tractate of *Chagigah* 12b. The first heaven, called the *vilon* (curtain) draws in every morning causing the light of day to become visible. In the evening it draws out and hides the daylight. The next heaven, the *rakia* (firmament) is that in which the sun and moon and constellations are set. The third heaven, called *shechakeem* (clouds) is that in which millstones stand and grind manna for the righteous. The fourth heaven, called *zevul* (lofty abode) is that in which the heavenly Jerusalem and Temple are built. The fifth heaven, *ma'on* (habitation) is that in which there are companies of ministering angels. *Makon* (fixed place), the sixth heaven, is that where there is stored the snow, hail, and rain. The last of the heavens, the *aravot* (thick darkness) is the place in which the souls of the righteous dwell.

There is also a mystical passage in the *Zohar* that provides the cause of the day's changing into night. In this passage, the earth is described as spinning in a circle like a ball, with one part up and the other down, one part light and the other dark, one part day and the other night. Amazingly, this mystical view antedated that of the great Copernicus by some 250 years!

MOTIONS OF THE HEAVENLY BODIES

The Talmud ascribes, as do most astronomers before the time of Copernicus, to the geocentric world conception, according to which the stars move about the earth. The *beraita* of the Talmud *Pesachim* 94b presents an early description of the various rabbinic viewpoints as they relate to the movement of heavenly bodies: "The learned of Israel say, 'The sphere stands firm, and the planets revolve.' The learned of the nations say: 'The spheres move, and the planets stand firm.' The learned of Israel say: 'The sun moves by day beneath the firmament and by night above the firmament.' The learned of the nations say: 'The sun moves by day beneath the firmament, and by night beneath the earth.' "

That the constant changes in the positions of the rising of the sun and its setting in the annual sun's cycle was well known in Talmudic times is evidenced from statements in the Jerusalem Talmud, *Rosh Hashanah* 2:5 and 58a, and Exodus Rabbah 15:22. In these texts it is reported that the sun has 365 windows through which it emerges: 182 in the east and 182 in the west, and one in the middle, the place of its first entrance. According to Genesis Rabbah 10:4, the sun completes its course in twelve months, Jupiter in twelve years, Saturn in thirty years, and Venus and Mars in 480 years.

Another solar motion concept is found in the *beraita* of the Talmud *Berachot* 59b, which explains the cycle of 28 years, at the end of which the sun returns to its original position relative to the stars and planets. The moon cycle of twenty-one years is mentioned in the text of Pirkei of Rabbi

Eliezer 7, and a hint of the nineteen-year cycle in the Targum Jonathan, commenting on Genesis 1:14.

THE *TEKUFOT* (SEASONS)

The four seasons of the year are known as the four *tekufot* or cycles. They are *tekufat* Nisan, the vernal equinox (March 21), when day and night are equal, the beginning of spring; *tekufat* Tammuz, the summer solstice (June 21), when the day is the longest in the year; *tekufat* Tishri, the autumnal equinox (September 23), when autumn begins and the day again equals the night; and *tekufat* Tevet, the winter solstice (December 22), the beginning of winter, when the night is the longest in the year. Changes of seasons are quite fully described in rabbinic times. The Midrash to the Book of Psalms 19:3 describes four seasons of the year, from the Nisan season to the Tammuz season the day borrows from the night, from the Tammuz season to the Tishri season the day repays the night, from the Tishri season to the Tevet season the night borrows from the day, and from the Tevet season to the Nisan and the Tishri season, neither one owes anything to the other. The Midrash of Genesis Rabbah 34:11 mentions six seasons of the year, and a reference to the receptacle of the sun by means of which the heat of the orb is mitigated appears in Genesis Rabbah 6:6.

According to the famous Babylonian Talmudic sage Mar Samuel, who was an expert astronomer, each *tekufah* marks the beginning of a period of ninety-one days and seven and a half hours. Because of his skill in regulating the calendar, he is generally referred to as *"Yarchina'ah"* (from the

Hebrew *yerach*—month). One of his famous sayings was: "The paths of the sky are as clear to me as the paths of Nehardea" (Talmud *Berachot* 58b).

The *Zohar*, the premier book in Jewish mysticism, contains a passage that presents as a reason for the day's changing into night the revolution of the earth. Long before Copernicus, the *Zohar* stated that "the whole earth spins in a circle like a ball; the one part is up when the other part is down; one part is light when the other is dark; it is day in the one part and night in the other."

THE ZODIAC

The names of the planets—Saturn (*Shabbetai*), Jupiter (*Tzedek*), Mars (*Maadim*), Sun (*Chamah*), Venus (*Kochevet* or *Noga*), Mercury (*Kochav*), and the Moon (*Levanah*) were referred to collectively as the acrostic **SHeTZM CHeNKaL** (Talmud *Shabbat* 129b, 156a). From the names of the seven planets were derived the names of the day of the week, and each day was consecrated to the specific planet that ruled during the early morning hours.

The twelvefold division of the zodiac was first developed by the Chaldean astronomers and was likely suggested by the occurrence of twelve full moons in successive parts of the heavens in the course of a calendar year. There is no mention of the zodiac in the Talmud, possibly due in part to the rabbinic statement of Jochanan (Talmud *Shabbat* 156a) based on the verse in Jeremiah 10:2 (Thus says God, do not learn the way of the nations and be not dismayed at the signs of heaven, for the nations are dismayed at them). Rabbi

Yochanan said that Israel is immune from the influence of the planets.

The zodiac is first mentioned in the book called *Sefer Yetzirah*, an eighth-century work considered to be the first written in Hebrew of speculative thought whose central theme is cosmology and cosmogony. The twelve signs of the zodiac, their Hebrew names (direct translations of the Latin names), and their relation to the months of the Jewish year are as follows:

1. Aries (*Taleh*, the lamb) for the month of Nisan.
2. Taurus (*Shor*, the ox) for the month of Iyar.
3. Gemini (*Teomim*, twins) for the month of Sivan.
4. Cancer (*Sarton*, crab) for the month of Tammuz.
5. Leo (*Ari*, lion) for the month of Av.
6. Virgo (*Betulah*, virgin) for the month of Elul.
7. Libra (*Maznayim*, scales) for the month of Tishri.
8. Scorpion (*Akrav*, scorpion) for the month of Cheshvan.
9. Sagittarius (*Kashat*, rainbow) for the month of Kislev.
10. Capricorn (*Gedi*, goat) for the month of Tevet.
11. Aquarius (*Deli*, vessel of water) for the month of Shevat.
12. Pisces (*Dagim*, fish) for the month of Adar.

As a memory device, the following acronym was created: **TeSHeT   SaAB   Ma'AK   GeDaD.**

According to the *Yalkut Shimoni* (a thirteenth-century midrashic compilation), the standards of the twelve tribes correspond to the twelve signs of the zodiac. Thus in the east were stationed Judah, Issachar, and Zebulun, corresponding to Aries, Taurus, and Gemini; Reuben, Simeon, and Gad in the south corresponding to Cancer, Leo, and Virgo; Ephraim, Manasseh, and Benjamin in the west corresponding to Libra, Scorpio, and Sagittarius; and Dan, Asher, and Naphtali in the north, corresponding to Capricorn, Aquarius, and Pisces. In the *Pesikta Rabbati*, a medieval midrash on the festivals of the year, a passage appears that explains the names of the zodiacal signs homiletically in accordance with Jewish history. Thus, for example, Taurus, whose sign is the ox, is connected with the calf that Abraham slaughtered for his angelic visitors (Genesis 18:7). Gemini represented the twin brothers Jacob and Esau. Regarding the Jerusalem Temple, it was said that it could not have been destroyed in the Hebrew month of Nisan, because the ram that it presents in the zodiac is a reminder of the binding of Isaac narrative. Furthermore, the reason why the Temple could be destroyed in the month of Av was that its zodiacal sign of the lion (*aryeh* in Hebrew) corresponds to Ariel, a name given to the Temple itself.

In 1928 when an irrigation channel was being dug in the Heftzai Bah kibbutz near Bet Alfa, a mosaic pavement was found by chance. Considered to be among the most important pieces of evidence available about synagogue architecture in the Byzantine period, the mosaic included a cosmological design portraying the sun god Helios in his chariot, which is drawn by four horses. All around it are shown the twelve signs of the zodiac, attesting to its importance in ancient Jewish art.

MORE HEAVENLY BODIES

Other heavenly bodies make their way into rabbinic literature as well. When Rabbi Jacob died, stars were seen by day, whereas when Rabbi Chiyya died, stones of fire descended from the heavens (Talmud *Moed Katan* 25b). These stones of fire may have referred to a meteor shower. The Milky Way is called "Fire-Stream," a name borrowed from the Book of Daniel 7:10 (*Nehar dinur*). There is also a statement in the Talmudic tractate of *Berachot* 58b, which states that the sting of Scorpio may be seen lying in the Milky Way. Samuel is quoted in the Jerusalem Talmud, *Berachot* 9:13c, that there is a tradition that no comet ever passed across the face of Orion, for if such a thing were to occur, the earth itself would be destroyed. Samuel is further quoted as stating that "but for warmth of Orion, the earth could not exist, because of the extreme cold of Scorpio."

The Aramaic term of a star that draws is *kocheva deshabi*. Whereas the medieval commentator Rashi understands this term to mean shooting star, Samuel states in the Talmud *Berachot* 58b that this is a comet, because of its tail. In the Talmudic tractate of *Horayot* (10a), Joshua ben Hananiah declared that a star appears once every seventy years and leads mariners astray. This necessitates that they should lay in a larger store of provisions. Some commentators believe that Joshua was likely referring to Halley's comet, the most famous one of them all, which passes close to the earth every seventy-six years, most recently in 1986.

Recently, Al Wolters, a Canadian professor of Bible studies, proposed an intriguing theory related to Halley's comet and the festival of Hanukkah. His theory attempts to explain the connection between Halley's comet, the brightest of the periodically returning comets, and its connection to Hanukkah, which has been called the Feast of Lights. According to astronomical calculations, Halley's comet was likely visible in Jerusalem at the time of the first Hanukkah in 164 B.C.E. At that time the comet was said to have come unusually close to the earth, within sixteen million kilometers. Its appearance then might well have made a spectacular display in the night sky at just about the time the Jews begin the process of the purification of the Temple. Thus according to Wolters, many Jewish people would have been struck by the coincidence of this great light in the heavens and the great liberation celebration in the festival of Hanukkah thereafter, thus calling the festival of dedication the Feast of Lights!

ASTRONOMY TODAY

The modern epoch of astronomical science begins with Sir William Herschel, a nineteenth-century Jew who systematically surveyed the heavens; his most significant discovery of the planet Uranus may be classified as one of the most important astronomical discoveries of the modern era. Outstanding Russian Jewish astronomists include Vitoli Lazarevich Gimzburg and Joseph Shkovsi, and leading French ones include Jean Claude Pecker, former general secretary of the International Astronomical Union and Evry Schatzman of the Parisian Astrophysics Institute.

Albert Einstein is noted for his research in astrophysics. Martin Schwarzschild, a professor at Princeton University, was an expert in the evolution of stars and telescope design. The originator of the so-called Big Bang Theory, a theory according to which the universe began billions of years ago in a single event, similar to an explosion, is the American Jewish scientist Arno Penzius. Cosmological and other astronomical work of great originality continues to develop, and it is likely that many more Jewish scientists will make significant contributions to the world of astronomy in the future.

ASTROLOGY

Astrology is generally said to refer to a study of the positions and relationships of the sun, moon, stars, and planets in order to judge their influence on human actions. Unlike astronomy, astrology is not a scientific study and has been much criticized by scientists. However, it clearly continues to be a part of the belief system of many people, judging by the popularity of horoscopes and fortune telling along with many books on the subject.

IN THE BIBLE AND THE APOCRYPHA

There is no precise mention of astrology in the Bible, although several biblical passages dealing with the diviner (in Hebrew *menachesh*) and soothsayer (in Hebrew, *me'onen*) appearing in Leviticus 19:26 and Deuteronomy 18:10 were understood by some of the rabbis as being correlated to astrology. Thus, in the Talmudic tractate of *Sanhedrin* 65b–66a, Rabbi Akiba interprets the *me'onen* to mean one who calculates times and hours for doing various tasks in life, while the rabbis are quoted as defining the *menachesh* in terms of good and bad omens.

The belief that planets and stars influenced the fate of human beings stemmed from ancient Babylonia. The Prophets of Israel were also aware of the customs and practices of the star gazers (in Hebrew *chovray ha-shamayaim*) among the Babylonians and other Near Eastern peoples, attacking their knowledge as futile and idolatrous. For instance, in the Book of Isaiah 47:13, the prophet is quoted as saying that the heaven scanners and star gazers will leave a person helpless. Daniel the Prophet refers to the astrologers as the Chaldeans, the ancient Semitic people well versed in divination and occult learning and casters of horoscopes.

The Apocryphal Book of Jubiless (12:16–18) describes Abraham the patriarch as overcoming the beliefs of astrologers, while the First Book of Enoch (8:3) includes astrology as one of the sins spread among humans by the primeval giants known as the *nefilim*.

IN THE TALMUD AND MIDRASH

There can be no doubt that Jews in ancient times did believe in astrology. Many Talmudic rabbis, for instance, are quoted as believing in it, although some of them held that the stars had no influence over Jews, who were under direct divine influence.

In the Babylonian Talmud, astrologers are known in

Hebrew as *kaldiyyim* (*Pesachim* 113b) and by the Aramaic term *kalda'ei* (Talmud *Shabbat* 119a and 156b). The Jerusalem Talmud more frequently uses the term "astrologiya" for the term astrology.

Many stories, parables, and quotations in the rabbinic writings reflect the wide range of views as related to astrology and its efficacy. The following is a brief summary of the many deliberations of the rabbinic sages.

Many of the Talmudic sages believed in the major role played by the heavenly bodies in the determination of human affairs in the sublunar world. In one instance Abraham and his progeny are spoken of as having been elevated beyond subjection to the stars (Genesis Rabbah 44:12), but on the other hand the blessing bestowed upon the patriarch in Genesis 24:1 is interpreted in the *Tosefta* of *Kiddushin* 5:17 as the gift of astrology.

Astrological consultation is one of the methods suggested by Jethro, father-in-law to Moses, for selecting the governing body of Israel (*Mechilta Amalek* 2). Here are several rabbinic parables from different astrological points of view:

A king who had no son said to his attendants, "Buy pen and ink for my son." The people took the king to be a great astrologer, for how could he have ordered pen and ink for his son had he not known beforehand that he was to have one? The same applies to God, who foresaw that He would at some future time give Israel the Torah. (Genesis Rabbah 1:4)

A ruler sentenced a man to death by fire. When he perceived by means of astrology that the condemned would beget a daughter destined to become the wife of the king, he said, "This man must be saved for his daughter's sake." Thus God did save Abraham from the fiery furnace, because of Jacob. (Leviticus Rabbah 36:4)

When Pharoah made Joseph vice regent, his astrologers asked, "Would you elevate this slave, purchased for twenty pieces of silver, to be ruler over us?" Pharoah answered, "I see the rulership in him." (Talmud *Sotah* 36b)

In reference to a request of King Solomon for laborers on the Temple, Pharoah asked his astrologers to select workers who were to die within the year and send them to the Jewish monarch, who, however, seeing the ploy through the medium of the Holy Spirit, sent them back again dressed in shrouds (*Pesikta* v, 34a).

According to the midrash (Genesis Rabbah 85:2), when a pagan wished to purchase a slave, he first consulted an astrologer. It was through astrology that Potiphar's wife learned that she was to have a son by Joseph, and it was for this reason that she regarded him with favor. It was, however, a grave error, for the prognostication referred to her daughter, who subsequently became Joseph's wife.

Several instances are cited in the Talmud of astrologers whose predictions of future events came true. For example, in the Talmudic tractate of *Shabbat* 119a, there is the famous story of a person called Joseph who always honored the Sabbath. Living near him was a rich gentile. One day an astrologer told the gentile that this man called Joseph would consume all of his property. So he went and sold all of his property and bought a precious jewel with the proceeds, which he placed in his turban. As he was crossing a bridge the wind blew the turban into the water and a fish swallowed it. Subsequently the fish was caught and brought to market on the eve of the Sabbath. Joseph, the man who always honored the Sabbath, bought it, opened it, and discovered the jewel. Thus the prediction of the astrologer indeed came true!

Traces of the ancient belief that stars can hold an influence over people can be found in words used by the ancient rabbis. The most familiar term is the expression "*mazal tov*," which is often today interpreted to mean good luck or good fortune. The phrase *mazal tov*, however, literally refers to "a good star." An unfortunate fellow today is still called a *shlimazal*—one who has no *mazal*, one on whom fortune does not smile. In several Talmudic passages it is stated that every person has a celestial body (i.e., a *mazal*), a particular star which is his or her patron from conception and from birth, and which perceives things unknown even to the person himself or herself. For example, the Talmudic tractate of *Shabbat* 53b discusses the planetary influence on human beings, whereas in the Talmudic tractate of *Megillah* 3a, it is stated that if a person is seized with fright (although he sees nothing) that his star sees, and the recitation of the *Shema* prayer is a remedy.

The Talmudic tractate of *Nedarim* 39b describes the phenomenon of two people born under the same star as sharing both a bodily and spiritual kinship, whereas the midrash of Genesis Rabbah 1:6 fully describes the connection of certain constellations of stars, including those of Pleiades and Orion, as influencing the growth and the ripening of fruits.

The stars of the proselytes were already witnesses of the revelation of Mount Sinai (Talmud *Shabbat* 146a), whereas the same tractate (53b) states that the reason that animals are more prone to injury is because they have no stars. On the other hand, every blade of grass (Genesis Rabbah 1:6) has its own particular star that proposes that it grow. According to the tractate *Berachot* 55b, the setting of one's personal star means that one's death is imminent.

The Pirke of Rabbi Eliezer 1 enhances the notion that astrologers were capable of controlling the planets. Thus, the malevolent Haman in the Book of Esther who set out to exterminate the entire Jewish community was said to have regulated the time for the extinction of the people by means of astrological calculations. An astrologer in the Talmudic tractate of *Shabbat* 156 predicted that a newborn male infant was destined to become a robber. For this reason, his mother always kept her child's head covered in order that the fear of heaven be upon him. Once, the covering fell from his head in his adult life, and he was said to have fulfilled the dire prediction of the astrologer by eating from a fruit tree that did not belong to him.

In spite of all the astrological predictions and citations in rabbinic writings, some rabbis continued to be skeptical of the ability of the astrologer to interpret the stars correctly, conceding the possibility that although one might well predict the future, the true understanding of the content of that forecast is likely to be in error. This hesitancy toward true astrological findings can be seen in the rabbinic quotation Talmud (*Sotah* 12b) that "the astrologers gaze but do not know at what they gaze, and they ponder and do not always know that which they are pondering."

Even the well-known Talmudic teacher, Samuel of Babylonia, one of the most adept of all ancient astrologers, quoting the words (Deuteronomy 30:12), "the Law is not in the heavens," says that "Torah cannot go together with the art that studies the heavens" (Deuteronomy Rabbah 8:6). An analogous remark is made in the Talmud *Pesachim* 113 by Jose of Hutzal who said that "we are not permitted to appeal to the Chaldeans [astronomers], for it is written [Deuteronomy 13:13] 'You shall be perfect with the Lord your God.'"

The *Shulchan Aruch*, Judaism's most authoritative law code, states categorically: "One should not consult astrologers nor should one cast lots in order to determine the future (Code of Jewish Law, *Yoreh Deah* 179:1).

Medieval Jewish scholars who were versed in astrology and considered it a true science include Saadia Gaon, whose commentary on *Sefer Yetzirah* contains astrological material, Solomon ibn Gabirol, whose *Keter Malchut* included an account of the influence of each of the seven planets, and Abraham ib Daud, whose book *Emunah Ramah* argues that the positions of the stars were set at the time of creation and that predictions can be made on the basis of them.

In one of the famous examples of the extraordinary independence of the mind of the medieval philosopher Moses Maimonides, he virtually alone rejected the belief in astrology. In a letter on astrology written in reply to a query from the rabbis of southern France, Maimonides distinguishes between astronomy, a true science, and astrology, which he deems as sheer superstition. He further states that according to the Torah a person's fate is determined directly by God and not by the stars. Despite his great prestige, Maimonides' criticism of astrology had little influence on subsequent Jewish writers.

Several Jewish astrologers served in various royal capitals in southern and western Europe. Among these were Judah ben Moses ha-Kohen at the court of Alfonso X of

Castile, Jacob Alcorsono and Crescas de Vivers at the courts of Pedro IV and John I of Aragon, and Abraham Zacuto at the court of Manuel I of Portugal.

ASTROLOGY AND KABBALAH

The mystical work *Sefer Yetzirah* contains several astrological passages of interest. One describes the relationship of the seven Hebrew consonants that take a *dagesh* to the seven planets and the seven days of the week, and the relationship of the twelve simple consonants to the twelve houses of the zodiac and the twelve months. In the *Sefer Raziel* the main basis for the systematic study of astrology is found. For instance, "How can the seers know what a person's life will be as soon as one is born? The ruling planet ascended in the East [at the hour of birth] is his wife's house. If the house of Saturn is in ascension, that person will live to be 57, if it is the house of Jupiter, one will live 79 years . . . Saturn presides over wealth and poverty . . . Jupiter rules over well-being, happiness, riches, honor, greatness and royalty. Mars presides over blood and the sword, Venus over attractiveness, grace and appetite . . ."

The mystical book of the *Zohar* takes astrology quite for granted. For example, it is stated (*Ki Tetze* 3, 281b, *Raya Meheimna*) that "all the stars and the constellations in the heavens were appointed to be rulers and commandments over the world. There is not even one single blade of grass in the entire world over which a star or a planet does not preside . . ."

In *Pinchas* 216b, it is stated that prior to the giving of the

Torah all earthly creatures were dependent on the stars. After the Sinai revelation, however, God exempted those Israelite children who studied and observed God's Law from the rule of the stars, whereas the skeptics and ignorant ones were not absolved.

HOROSCOPES AND SELECTION OF DAYS

One of the most popular forms of astrological folklore and superstition is the selection of lucky days. According to it, certain periods, years, months, days, and hours are regarded as either lucky or unlucky. The following is a summary of rabbinic opinion that describes the vestiges of astrology in Jewish folklore:

1. No business should begin on the new moon, on Friday, or on the Sabbath evening (*Sifra, Kedoshim* 6).

2. It is dangerous to drink water on Wednesday and Friday evenings (Talmud *Pesachim* 112a).

3. It is dangerous to bleed a patient on Monday, Tuesday, or Thursday, because on the last mentioned day Mars reigns at the even numbered hours of the day, when demons have their play (Talmud *Shabbat* 129b).

4. It is dangerous to undergo an operation on a Wednesday falling on the fourth, the fourteenth, or the twenty-fourth of the month, or on a Wednesday occurring within less than four days of the new moon (Talmud *Shabbat* 129b).

5. One should perform marriages only in the first half of the month while the moon was waxing (Nachmonides, responsum no. 282).

6. The custom of fasting on the anniversary of a parent's death is derived from the belief that on that day the luck of the child is vulnerable (Rabbi Mordecai Jaffe, commenting on Isserles to Code of Jewish Law, *Yoreh Deah* 402:12).

7. Men born on Sunday will be distinguished; on Monday, wrathful; on Tuesday, wealthy and sensual; on Wednesday, intelligent and enlightened; on Thursday, benevolent, on Friday, pious. Those born on Saturday are destined to die on that day (Horoscope of Joshua ben Levi).

8. Rabbi Haninah said: Those born while the sun rules in the heavens will have a brilliant career, and they will eat and drink of their own substance. But their secrets will be divulged and they will never prosper by theft. Those born under the dominion of Venus are destined to wealth and sensual enjoyment, because fire is suspended on this star. Being born under the planet of Mercury forecasts intelligence and enlightenment. Those born under the reign of the moon will suffer much sorrow. The plans of those born under the reign of Saturn will be destroyed, while the righteous and charitable people are born under the reign of Jupiter. The shedder of blood is born under the influence of Mars (Talmud *Shabbat* 156a).

9. On joyful occasions Jewish people everywhere continue to congratulate each other by saying "*mazal tov.*" A successful person is often called a *bar-mazal* (one having good fortune), a perennial failure may be called a *ramazal*, while an unfortunate person is called a *shlimazal*.

10. An unslept-in bed (called the bed of Gad) in a house is a good luck charm (Talmud *Moed Katan* 27a). The astrological custom was forgotten and the noun "*gad*," originally the name of a star, came to simply mean "luck."

DIVINATION AND SORCERY

IN THE BIBLE

Since time immemorial humans have longed to learn that which the future holds for them. Thus, in ancient civilizations, and even today with fortune telling as a true profession, humankind continues to be curious about its future, both out of sheer curiosity as well as out of desire to better prepare for it.

The forecasting of the future by certains signs or movements of external things has come to be known as *divination*. Many ancient people believed that the prediction of the future was possible, and that it was bound up with superhuman, demonic, or divine power from which the diviner received knowledge. The belief seemed to be that *either* certain persons had natural talents for receiving future forecasts, and others predicted future events through signs whose interpretations had to be learned. The Mesopotamians had their own special brand of fortune tellers, whereas Egyptian documents indicate that diviners served both individuals as well as the Pharaoh.

In a God-fearing Israel, everything was to be based on the will and spirit of God. The Bible expressly forbids any form of divination, considering it an idolatrous practice:

> Neither shall you use enchantments nor practice augury. Do not turn to them that have familiar spirits or to the wizards (Leviticus 19:26, 31). There shall not be found with you . . . one that uses divination, one that practices augury, or an enchanter, or a sorcerer, or a charmer, or a consulter with a familiar spirit, or a wizard or a necromancer.
>
> One does these things as an abomination to God, and because of these abominations 'Adonai your God does drive them out from before you.' " (Deuteronomy 17:10–11)

Various forms of divination did exist in biblical times. This chapter delineates several proper means by which the Israelites were allowed to inquire into the future.

The general term for divination in Hebrew is *"kesem."* The elders of Moab and Midian are described as versed in divination in the Book of Numbers 22:7. The original meaning of *kesem* has been said to connect to a verse in the Book of Ezekiel 26:21, where King Nebuchadnezzar is represented as standing at the parting of the ways and shaking arrows to determine the direction of his travel— either toward Jerusalem or to the Ammonite capital. Thus the word *kasam* is said to derive from the Arabic word *istaksam*, meaning to obtain a divine decision.

Specific forms of divination are mentioned in the Book of Leviticus 19:26 as being expressly forbidden to the Israelite. These include various mourning customs connected with the heathen worship of the dead, including self-mutilation and shedding of blood, believed to have had a sacrificial value for the dead person.

The Bible mentions that the so-called *Urim* and *Thummim* were consulted in order to determine the needs of the community (Numbers 27:21 and I Samuel 14:41). The *Urim* and *Thummim* (light and perfection) were two mysterious objects contained in the breastplate of the high priest. First mentioned in the Book of Exodus 28:30, it is stated that "you shall place the *Urim* and *Thummim* in the breastplate of judgment, that they may be over Aaron's heart whenever he enters God's Presence."

Because the exact nature of the *Urim* and *Thummim* is uncertain, various explanations have been offered. One suggests that they were lots of some kind that were drawn or cast by the high priest to ascertain God's decision in doubtful matters of national importance. Used until the reign of King Solomon, the *Urim* and *Thummim* were later abandoned in favor of advice given by the prophets.

The breastplate of judgment (in Hebrew, *choshen hamishpat*) bore the names of Israel's tribes on twelve precious stones. The gleaming of the gems in the breastplate, according to some commentators, miraculously confirmed the answer that occurred to the high priest while he was offering prayer for divine guidance. Others are of the opinion that the answer was inward illumination, without any external sign. In his great faith, the high priest believed that the response that dawned in his mind was divinely inspired and therefore correct.

Among the masses it was also a widespread practice to seek false prophets and fortune tellers, as is ascertained from the various disputes of the true prophets against them. For instance, in the Book of Ezekiel 13:17, Ezekiel is cautioned to set his face against those who prophesy "out of their imagination."

In some instances in the Bible, the true Israelite prophets were to perform the function of the mantic who foretells of the future. For example, in the Book of Deuteronomy 18:14, we learn that the nations that Israel is about to dispossess do indeed resort to soothsayers and augurs. However, the Israelites are assured that God will choose prophets in whose mouths will be placed His words, and these will speak on their behalf. But any prophet who presumes to speak in God's name an oracle that God did not authorize will be put to death. Thus the criterion given for distinguishing between a true and a false prophet is the fulfilment of the prophecy.

Israelite prophets were often consulted on matters of a type that a soothsayer would answer. Thus in the story of King Saul and the asses, Samuel's servant is quoted as saying to the seer: "All that he says comes true" (I Samuel 9:6). Jeroboam sent his wife to Ahijah of Shiloh (I Kings 14:1) to inquire whether his son would live.

METHODS OF FORETELLING THE FUTURE IN THE BIBLE: OMENS

The simplest means of foretelling the future was through the ability to interpret natural signs and omens. The Hebrew word *menachesh* is used as the general term for one who observes omens. For example, in the Book of Genesis 44:5 a divining cup is described as Joseph sets forth a test to ascertain the sincerity of his brothers. Such divining goblets were often used in Egypt. Pieces of gold or silver were thrown into water or liquid in the goblet and caused movements, which were supposed to represent coming events. This type of divination was also known to the Romans, Chaldeans, and Babylonians.

Another form of divination was the casting of rods. Reference to divination rods is made in the Book of Hosea 4:6: "My people ask counsel at their stock, and their staff declares to them." Divination by arrows (whose technical name is balomancy) is explicitly mentioned in the Book of Ezekiel 21:26, in which King Nebuchadnezzar is described as shaking the arrows while consulting the *teraphim*. Divination was said to be practiced by some Aram tribes and Mesopotamian documents have confirmed the practice of casting lots by flinging arrows into a quiver.

Consultation of *teraphim* (i.e., images of domestic deities used for divination) is also mentioned in connection with foretelling of the future. For instance, in the Book of Zechariah 10:2, we learn of the futility of consulting the *teraphim* as the text states that "the *teraphim* spoke delusion."

The Bible mentions a type of foretelling of the future by which an interpretation was given to a conventional word that was seen as a sign. This type of divination is described in the Book of Samuel I, 14:9–10, in the story of Jonathan and his battle with the Philistines: "If they say to us, 'wait until we come to you,' then we will stand in our place, and we will not go up to them. But if they say 'come up to us,' then we will go up; for God has given them into our hand. And this shall be the sign to us."

The study of the liver, often regarded as the seat of life, is mentioned in the Book of Ezekiel 21:26 as a means of divination. The diviner inspected the internal organs of the animal in a prescribed and organized manner, and from its signs was able to prognosticate the future.

The ancient art of calling up dead spirits (known as necromancy) was also well known in biblical times. Although forbidden by biblical law, diviners do appear in the Bible who are connected with the consultation of dead spirits. For example, in the Book of Isaiah 19:3, mention is made of those who seek ghosts and the dead spirits. King Saul himself resorted to consulting his deceased mentor, Samuel, through the medium of the famous witch of Endor (I Samuel 28:7).

Other even more sophisticated methods of divination include dream interpretation and astrology, each of which are dealt with in great detail in separate chapters of this volume.

DIVINATION IN THE TALMUD

The rabbis adopted an attitude of mixed opinions regarding divination. Clearly, they realized that divination was expressly forbidden in the Bible. On the other hand, because the Babylonian scholar lived in an environment where divination was widely practiced, they offered various opinions on the subject often related to the distinction between divination proper and signs of the future, which were permissible.

For example, the *Sifra Kedushim* 6 discusses divination by "weasels, birds and stars," referring to the cries of these animals and the courses of the stars in the sky. The *Sifrei* of Deuteronomy 171 suggests graphic examples of people regulating their conduct by means of omens. For example, "if he says that bread has fallen from his mouth, his staff from his hand, a snake passed on his right and a fox on his left and his tail crossed his path [these are bad omens], or if he refuses to do something because it is the New Moon or the eve of the Sabbath or Saturday night." The Talmudic tractate of *Sanhedrin* 65 adds the croaking of a raven at a man or the crossing of a deer on his path as additional evil omens.

The dividing line between divination and legitimate signs is indicated by the statement "any divination which is not as the divination of Eliezer the servant of Abraham at the well [Genesis 24:14] or Jonathan the son of Saul [I Samuel 14:9–10] is no divination" (Talmud *Chullin* 95b). Rabbinic interpretations regarding this statement include those stating that divinations of the kind described above are permitted, whereas others state emphatically that they are forbidden.

Another statement in the Talmudic tractate of *Chullin* 95b states that "a house, child and a wife, though they do not constitute divination, do act as signs." The importance of this statement is that good or bad luck that immediately follows a house purchase, a child's birth, or marriage may be understood as omens of success or failure.

Another kind of permissible divination in the Talmud was the custom of asking a child to recite his biblical verse. In the Talmudic tractate of *Chullin* 95b, Rabbi Jochanan decided to visit Samuel in Babylon after the death of Rav. He asked a child to quote his verse and the child recited

"Now Samuel was dead" (I Samuel 28:3). Jonathan subsequently took this as a sign but the Talmud adds, "it was not so. It was only that Jochanan should not be put to the trouble of visiting him." Another Talmudic passage (*Bava Batra* 12b) goes on to say that "if a person wakes up to find that a scriptural verse has fallen into his mouth, it is a minor prophecy."

Sometimes the distinction between divination and signs was extremely fine. When Rav went on a journey and came to a ford, if he saw the ferryboat coming toward him he regarded it as a good omen, and if it was departing from him he regarded it as an evil omen (Talmud *Chullin* 95b). Jochanan ben Zakkai was reported to have knowledge of the language of palm trees (Talmud *Sukkah* 28a).

In general, one could say that the view of the rabbinic authorities to divination is that although it might be possible for certain "gifted" persons to foretell the future, one ought to refrain from such practices and trust in God's judgment.

NOTABLE QUOTATIONS
RELATED TO DIVINATION

The following is a cross-section of statements and quotations from rabbinic sources that shed additional light on the ancient practice of divination:

1. Ten measures of witchcraft came down to the world. The Egyptians took nine, and the rest of the world, all of it, took one (Talmud *Kiddushin* 49b).

2. When a woman sought to take earth from under Rabbi Haninah's feet [in order to bewitch him], he said to her, "If you can do it, go and practice your sorcery, but remember Scripture's warning: 'There is no one beside Him.'"

But is that really so? Did not Rabbi Yochanan say, "Why are sorcerers called *machshefim*? Because they diminish the power of the household above?" However, Rabbi Haninah is different, because his merit is so abundant (Talmud *Sanhedrin* 67b).

3. A *baal ov* [Leviticus 19:31] is a ventriloquist who speaks out of his armpit. The *yiddeoni*, "wizard," is one who puts a bone of the *yiddoa* in his mouth and speaks out of this bone (Talmud *Sanhedrin* 65a–65b).

4. Three things have been said about the one who brings up a dead person: One who brings him up sees him but does not hear his voice; one who needs him hears his voice but does not see him; and one who does not need him neither sees nor hears his voice (Leviticus Rabbah 26:7).

5. Our masters taught: A *meonen* is, according to Rabbi Simeon, one who applies the semen of seven species to his eyes in order to perform witchcraft. According to the sages, he is one who causes an optical illusion (*Sifre* Deuteronomy 171).

6. We have been taught: In the words "or that consults the dead" [Deuteronomy 18:11], Scripture refers to him who starves himself and then spends the night in a cemetery, so that an unclean spirit may rest upon him [to allow him to hear what the dead speak]. Whenever Rabbi Akiva reached this verse, he would burst into tears and say: "If an unclean spirit does come to rest on a person who fasts in order that it should do so, how much more and more should the desire be fulfilled of him who fasts in order that the pure spirit of the Divine Presence rest upon him. But alas, our sins have driven it away from us, as it is written, 'Your transgressions have been a barrier between you and your God'" [Isaiah 59:2] (Talmud *Sanhedrin* 65b).

7. When two women sit at a crossroads, one on one side and one on the other, facing one another, it is clear that they are engaged in witchcraft. What is the remedy? If there is another road, let the traveler take it. If there is no other road, then, if another person is with him, let the two hold each other's hands and pass. If there is no other person, let the traveler say, "Agrat, Ozlat, Usia, Belusia have been slain with a dark arrow" (Talmud *Pesachim* 111a).

8. Yochani, daughter of Retivi, was a widowed witch. Whenever a woman's time to give birth had arrived, Yochani would shut the woman's womb by witchcraft. After the woman had suffered greatly, the witch would say, "I will go and implore God's mercy. Perhaps my prayer will be heard." She went and undid her witchcraft, and the child was born. Once, when she went to the house of a woman about to give birth, leaving behind in her own house a man hired by the day, the hired man heard the sound of witchcraft knocking about in a vessel, as an embryo is knocked about in its mother's womb. When he removed the vessel's stopper, the witcheries went out, and the child was born. Then all knew that the widow was a mistress of witchcraft (Rashi's commentary on the Talmud *Sotah* 22b).

9. The more women, the more witchcraft (*Pirke Avot*, 2:7).

OMENS IN THE MIDDLE AGES

During the Middle Ages, both Jews and Christians were taking and reading omens from bodily phenomena. Here is a brief summary of these omen indicators:

1. If the flesh under one's armpit quivers, they will be broaching a match to him soon. If the sole of one's foot itches, one will be journeying soon to a strange place (*Chochmat HaNefesh* 25d).

2. Sneezing during prayers is a good sign, and letting wind, a bad sign.

3. A dog howling mournfully is a sign that the angel of death is in town.

4. It is unlucky to open the day or the week with an action involving a loss. Thus it was considered undesirable to pay the tax collector on the first day of the week.

5. A seminal pollution on Yom Kippur was considered an omen of death.

6. Dropping a Bible on the ground was considered such a bad omen that even today it is customary to fast in order to make amends.

7. In the Rhineland it was believed that when the flames on the hearth leap high that a guest will soon arrive. If the fire is doused with water, the visitor will be drowned (Talmud *Yoma* 88a).

8. A snail burrowing in a house is an omen that an adulterous act will soon be committed there.

9. Eating pomegranates for the New Year will portend of fertility and good things.

10. Avoid eating nuts at the New Year, since the Hebrew word for nut, *egoz*, has the same numerical value of *chet* (i.e., sin).

11. Eating apples dipped in honey for the New Year, a custom that is still followed today, was a sign of a prosperous and sweet year.

12. Making a mistake in one's prayers is a sign of disaster.

13. Rabbi Ammi said: One who wishes to ascertain whether he will live through the year or not should, during the ten days between Rosh Hashanah and Yom Kippur, kindle a lamp in a house where there is no draft. If the light continues to burn, he may be certain that he will live through the year (Talmud *Horayot* 12a).

14. One who wishes to engage in business and wants to ascertain whether he will succeed or not should rear a cock; if it grows plump and handsome, he will succeed (Talmud *Horayot* 12a).

15. One who wishes to set out on a journey and wants to ascertain whether he will return to his home safely or not should stand in a dark house. If he sees the reflection of his shadow, he may be certain that he will return to his home safely. However, such a procedure is not desirable, for his courage may fail him, and in consequence he may meet with misfortune (Talmud *Horayot* 12a).

16. One who takes sick should not speak of it the first day, lest his luck turn worse. After the first day, he may speak freely of his sickness (Talmud *Berachot* 55b).

17. Our masters taught: When dogs howl, the angel of death has come to the city. When dogs frolic, the prophet Elijah has come to the city. This is so, however, only when there is no bitch among the dogs (Talmud *Baba Kamma* 60b).

18. Rabbi Isaac: He who wishes to become wise should turn southward when praying; and he who wishes to become rich should turn northward when praying. Why think so? In the tabernacle, the table [symbol of plenty] is in the north and the lampstand [symbol of wisdom] is in the south. But Rabbi Joshua ben Levi said: One should always turn in prayer to the south, for when one becomes wise, he is also likely to become rich, as it is said, Length of days is in wisdom's right hand; in her left hand are riches and honor [Proverbs 3:16] (Talmud *Bava Batra* 25b).

THE PROGNOSTIC ARTS

Knowing the future was not only satisfied through interpreting omens. Being proactive and creating one's own signs and portents was also practiced. Such practices in medieval times included the following:

1. Place a lighted candle during the Ten Days of Repentance (days between Rosh Hashanah and Yom Kippur) where no wind could extinguish it. If the light did go out, the person who lit it would die before year's end. If the candle burned in its entirety, then that person could count on at least one more year of life.

2. On the night of Hoshanna Rabbah (traditionally when God's Book of Life is officially sealed), go out into the moonlight to see if the shadows cast were lacking heads. The absence of a head was a sign that what would happen to the shadow would similarly occur with the body.

3. Open the Bible at random and take as a sign the first word or sentence that meets the eye. A variation of this practice was to ask children what verses they have studied in school that day and to take the verses as good or bad omens.

4. Cast lots by throwing dice or tossing a coin.

5. Ask a young child to gaze into a reflecting surface until the child saw figures that revealed the desired information.

6. It was a medieval belief that a treasure lay buried in the earth. Use a divining rod (a type of forked stick) along with certain incantations to discover the treasure. There are still people today who use such divining rods in order to find springs of water.

MAGIC

IN THE BIBLE

Magic generally refers to the art that purports to control or forecast natural events, effects, or forces by invoking the supernatural. What distinguishes magic from divination is the fact that divination only attempts to predict future events, whereas magic also professes to influence and change them for good or bad. Charms, spells, and rituals are often employed in order to achieve these supernatural events and to control events in nature. Black magic usually refers to mischievous illegal magic, whereas white magic refers to beneficent magic whose purpose is to protect against the forces of evil magic.

Interest in magic permeated the ancient Near East. Egypt, for example, was permeated with magical beliefs, and magic was called upon at every turn in life: to ward off dead spirits, demons, scorpions, serpents, and wildbeasts; to protect women in childbirth and newborn infants; and to ensure the dying person happiness beyond the grave.

For the Israelites, the most complete and detailed list of various kinds of practioners of magic occurs in chapter 18 of the Book of Deuteronomy, verses 10–11:

Let no one be found among you who consigns his son or daughter to the fire, or who is an augur, a soothsayer, an enchanter, or sorcerer. One who casts spells or one who consults ghosts or familiar spirits, or one who inquires of the dead. For any person who does such things is abhorrent to God . . .

Understanding of the terms used in these verses differ because it is difficult to determine with precision the practices to which the terms refer. Here is a brief summary of these terms and their possible interpretations:

1. One who consigns his son or daughter to the fire (in Hebrew, *maavir beno uvito ba'esh*): This phrase has often been taken to refer both to child sacrifice and to a type of oracle ordeal associated with divination and magic.

2. Augur (in Hebrew, *kosem kesameem*): This term is understood to refer to the whole complex of magical and divinatory practices in ancient Israel.

3. Soothsayer (in Hebrew, *me'onen*): This term has often come to be understood as a type of observer of the times, a person who looks for omens and practices divinatory ritual such as observation of the clouds, the so-called evil eye, as well as magical practices such as conjuring up spirits.

4. Enchanter (in Hebrew, *menachesh*): There is a debate as to the exact root of this word. Some commentators connect it with the root *Nchsh* (snake) and associate it with some form of divination related to snakes. Those emphasizing its connection with the root *lchsh* tend to associate it more with magic, particularly with the use of charms and enchantments.

5. Sorcerer (in Hebrew, *mechashef*): There is a general agreement regarding the meaning of this term, in which it usually refers to a type of witchcraft that uses supernatural power over others through the assistance of the spirits.

6. One who casts spells (in Hebrew, *chover chaver*): This term refers to a charmer, one who casts spells or uses charms. Some interpreters relate this concept to the practice of tying or wrapping magical knots or threads around people or objects, understood either to bind the gods to do one's will or to bind the object or person to be affected. Another interpretation relates the term to the idea that words are woven together in the spell itself. Still another interpretation relates this term to mutterer, one who makes indistinguishable clamor.

7. One who consults ghosts (in Hebrew, *sho'el ov ve'yidonee*): This term has often been understood to refer to a medium or a wizard, one who traffics with ghosts and spirits and has the ability to consult them.

8. One who inquires of the dead (in Hebrew, *doresh ha-meteem*): This term refers to the necromancer, one who calls up to the dead. However, the precise method by which this was done is unclear.

The Bible prohibits the practice of magic or presents it negatively in a number of places other than the reference in

Deuteronomy 18:10–11. Other references of prohibition include Leviticus 19:26, 31, Leviticus 20:1–6, Exodus 22:17, Isaiah 8:19, Isaiah 57:3, Ezekiel 22:28, and Malachi 3:5. Any belief in the efficacy of magic is seen as contradicting the Israelite belief in the supreme rule of the One God and thus viewed as an abomination. Witchcraft and divination using *teraphim* are identified with rebellion in I Samuel 15:23, sorcerers are described as pure vanity in Isaiah 47:8–15. Whereas the magicians of Egypt employ their secret arts in turning a rod into a snake, Moses and Aaron perform a similar stunt at the command of God. Ezekiel's denunciation of the sorceresses and their sympathetic magic practices is most profound:

> You, O mortal, set your face against the women of your people who prophesy out of their own imagination. Prophesy against them and say: Thus said the Lord God: Woe to all who sew pads on all arm joints and make bonnets for the head of every person in order to entrap. Can you hunt down lives among My people while you preserve your own lives? You have profaned My name among My people in return for handfuls of barley and morsels of bread. You have announced the death of persons who will not die and the survival of persons who will not live—lying to My people who listen to your lies. (Ezekiel 13:17–19)

Biblical law did not eradicate sorcery and magic, as can be attested to by the fact that prophets were constantly condemning them. For example, Isaiah (3:2–3), speaking in the name of God, says that all augurs and enchanters will be removed from Jerusalem and Judah. In the Book of Chronicles II:33:6, King Josiah is described as removing from Judah all of those who divined by a ghost or a familiar spirit.

IN THE APOCRYPHA

The Apocrypha, containing the religious writings that are noncanonical, generally present an attitude toward magic that is similar in nature to that of both the Bible and the Talmud. According to the Book of Enoch (9:7), the angels taught the daughters of men "incantations, exorcisms, and the cutting of roots, and revealed to them healing plants." The Second Book of Maccabees (12:40) tells of the Jewish warriors who kept amulets taken from the idols of Jamnia under their tunics.

In the Book of Tobit, the angel Raphael teaches Tobit's son that the smoke of a burning heart and liver from a certain fish cures a person possessed of a demon and the anointing of the eyes of a blind person with the gall of the same fish restores his eyesight (Tobit 6:5, 8:2–3, 11:10–11). In addition, Noah's book of healing (Jubilees 10) was magical in character.

IN THE TALMUD

The prohibition of magic that one finds in the Bible also finds expression in numerous places in the Talmud. Mishnah 7:7 of the Talmudic tractate of *Sanhedrin* equates magic with idolatry. In the Talmudic tractate of *Shabbat* 6:10, magical

remedies are denounced as being the custom of the Amorites. In the tractate of *Sanhedrin* (10:1), we are told that a
person who pronounces a magic formula over a wound loses
his share in the world to come.

Here are some selected statements from the Talmud
related to incidents of magic. They reflect the negative
feelings toward magical procedure.

1. Only a person who believes in the interpretation of
signs is pursued by magic (Talmud *Nedarim* 32a).

2. One who is free from superstition attains an eminence
in the world to come that is beyond the reach of the serving
angel (Talmud *Nedarim* 32a).

3. Harlotry and magic have caused the destruction of all
(Talmud *Sotah* 48a).

4. One who acquires a single item of knowledge from a
magician forfeits his life (Talmud *Shabbat* 75a).

5. Adultery and sorcery have destroyed everything
(Talmud *Sotah* 9:13).

There are a number of persons mentioned in the Talmud
who engaged in some sort of magic. For example, in the
Talmudic tractate of *Gittin* 45a, Rav Nachman's daughters
who were experienced in magical procedure were able to
stir a pot of boiling water with their bare hands. The widow
Yochani, a faith healer of Jerusalem, was able to delay a
birth by magical means. Perhaps one of the greatest magicians of them all, Choni ha-Me'aggel (i.e., the drawer of
circles), was able to use the drawing of circles (clearly an

act of magic) to bring about rain in time of drought. A contemporary of his, Shimon ben Shetach, who sought to eradicate magic, was quoted as saying in the Talmudic tractate of *Taanit* 19a "that if you were not Choni, whom God loves as a son, I would excommunicate you."

Healing in the Talmud by means of white magic is not condemned except when the means employed are pagan or idolatrous. Many scholars were able to consume men with a glance, or reduce them to a heap of bones, but since this magic was regarded as a punishment for transgressions that had been committed, their work seems to be permitted.

MAGIC PROCEDURE: BIBLICAL MAGIC VERSES

Biblical verses that were used for magical purposes included those that contained God's name or spoke of God's power and those that seemed to have more or less direct bearing on the immediate situation in which they were employed.

The Book of Psalms was considered an especially potent book for magical purposes. Perhaps the most popular book on the subject of magic using Psalms is the work entitled *Shimmush Tehillim* (The Use of Psalms). Written in the mid 1500s, its opening line states that "the entire Torah is composed of the names of God, and in consequence it has the property of saving and protecting man." The work quotes a tradition that when a particular town or city is endangered, it can be saved by reciting in order those Psalms whose initial letters spell out the name of the city.

Another work, entitled *Sefer Gematriaot*, lists a series of biblical verses and their magical use. Although some of these verses were recited as they are found in the Bible, others were recited by reversing the usual order, transposing words, or repeating them a given number of times. Sometimes the words were dissolved in a liquid and drunk, or worn on the person as an amulet. The following is a partial listing of the magical verses as listed in the book *Sefer Gematriaot*:

1. For a child who has been recently circumcised: So he blessed them that day saying, "By you shall Israel invoke blessings, saying: God make you like Ephraim and Manasseh." (Genesis 48:20)

2. To drive off evil spirits and demons, recite the following upon retiring to sleep: The Lord bless you and protect you. The Lord deal kindly and graciously with you. The Lord bestow His favor upon you and grant you peace. (Numbers 6:24–26)

3. To counteract magic: Recite the following ten verses, all of which begin and end with the Hebrew letter *nun*, in this order:

    i. When a person has a scaly affection, it shall be reported to the priest (*kohen*). Leviticus 13:9

    ii. We ourselves will cross over as shock-troops, at the instance of God, into the land of Canaan; and we shall keep our hereditary holding across the Jordan (*yarden*). Numbers 32:32

    iii. The Lord your God will raise up for you a prophet from among your own people, like myself; him you shall heed (*teeschma'un*). Deuteronomy 18:15

iv. Sweetness drops from your lips, O bride, honey and milk are under your tongue; the scent of your robes is like the scent of Lebanon (*levanon*). Song of Songs 4:11

v. I have sprinkled my bed with myrrh, aloes and cinnamon (*vekeenamon*). Proverbs 7:17

vi. The lifebreath of man is the lamp of the Lord, revealing all of his most innerparts (*chadray vaten*). Proverbs 20:27

vii. They were armed with the bow and could use both right hand and left hand to sling stones or shoot arrows with the bow; they were kinsmen of Saul from Benjamin (*binyameen*). I Chronicles 12:2

viii. Flee from Babylon, leave the land of the Chaldeans and be like he-goats that lead the flock (*tzon*). Jeremiah 50:8

ix. He performed wonders in the sight of their ancestors in the land of Egypt, the plain of Zoan (*tzo'an*). Psalm 78:12

x. You led Your people like a flock in the care of Moses and Aaron (*Aaron*). Psalm 77:21

4. To gain a good name: You are fair, my darling, you are fair, with your dove-like eyes. (Song of Songs 6:4–9)

5. To win credibility in an argument: Give ear, O heavens, let me speak; let the earth hear the words that I utter. May my speech come down as rain, my speech distill as the dew, like showers on young growth, like droplets on the grass. (Deuteronomy 32:1–2)

6. To have one's prayer answered: The Lord passed before him and proclaimed: "The Lord, the Lord—a God compassionate and gracious, slow to anger, abounding in kindness and faithfulness, extending kindness to the thousandth generation, forgiving iniquity, transgression and sin; yet God does not remit all punishment, visiting the iniquity of parents upon children and children's children, upon the third and fourth generations. (Exodus 34:6–7)

7. For a melodious voice: Then Moses and the Israelites sang this song to God. They said: I will sing to God, for He has triumphed gloriously. Horse and driver He has hurled into the sea. (Exodus 15:1)

8. To strengthen one's voice: Then Judah went up to him and said, "Please my lord, let your servant appeal to my lord, and do not be impatient with your servant, you who are the equal of Pharoah." (Genesis 44:18)

9. For a prayer leader: Who is she that shines through like the dawn, beautiful as the moon and radiant as the sun, awesome as bannered hosts. I went down to the nut grove to see the budding of the vale and to see if the vines had blossomed and if the pomegranates were in bloom. Before I knew it my desire set me amid the chariots of Amminadib. Turn back, turn back, O maid of Shulem. Turn back, turn back, that we may gaze upon you. "Why will you gaze at the Shulammite in the Machanaim dance?" How lovely are your feet in sandals O daughter of nobles. Your rounded thighs are like jewels, the work of a master's hand. Your navel is like a round goblet. Let mixed wine not be lacking. Your belly is like a heap of wheat hedged about with lilies. Your breasts are like two fawns, twins of a gazelle. Your neck is like a tower of ivory, your eyes like pools in Cheshbon by the gate of Bat-rabbim. Your nose is like the tower of Lebanon that faces toward Damascus. The head upon you is like crimson wool, the locks of your head are like purple. A king is held captive in the tresses. How fair you are, how beautiful. O love, with all its rapture. Your stately form is like the palm, your breasts are like clusters. I say: Let me climb the palm, let me take hold of its branches. Let your breasts be like clusters of grapes, your breath like the fragrance of apples, and your mouth like choicest wine. Let it flow to my beloved as new wine, gliding over the lips of sleepers. I am my beloved's, and my beloved is mine. (Song of Songs 6:10–7:11)

10. To arouse love: Your ointments yield a sweet fragrance, your name is like finest oil. Therefore do maidens love you. (Song of Songs 1:3)

11. At a marriage: You are fair, my darling. You are fair. Your eyes are like doves behind your veil. Your hair is like a flock of goats streaming down Mount Gilead. Your teeth are like a flock of ewes climbing up from the washing pool. All of them bear twins and not one loses her young. Your lips are like crimson thread, your mother is lovely. Your brow behind your veil shines like an open pomegranate. Your neck is like David's tower, built to hold weapons. It is hung with a thousand shields, all the quivers of warriors. Your breasts are like two fawns, twins of a gazelle, browsing among the lilies. When the day blows softly and the shadows flee, I will betake me to the mount of myrrh, to the hill of frankincense. Every part of you is fair, my darling, and there is no blemish in you. From Lebanon come with me. From Lebanon, my bride, come with me. Trip down from Amana's peak, from the peak of Senir and Chermon, from the dens of lions and from the hills of leopards. You have captured my heart, my own, my bride. You have captured my heart with one glance of your eyes, with one coil of your necklace. How sweet is your love, my own, my bride. How much more delightful your love than wine, your ointments more fragrant than any spice. Sweetness drops from your lips, O bride. Honey and milk are under your tongue, and the scent of your robes is like the scent of Lebanon. A garden locked is my own, my bride. A fountain locked, a sealed-up spring. Your limbs are an orchard of pomegranates and of all appetizing fruits, of henna and of nard. Nard and saffron, fragrant reed and cinnamon, with all aromatic woods. Myrrh and aloes, all the choice perfumes. You are a garden spring, a well of fresh water, a rill of Lebanon. Awake, O north wind, come, O south wind. Blow upon my garden, that its perfume may spread. Let my beloved come to his garden and enjoy its luscious fruits. I have come to my garden, my own, my bride. I have plucked my myrrh and spice, eaten my honey and honeycomb, drunk my wine and milk. Eat, lovers, and drink. Drink deep of love. I was asleep, but my heart was awake. Hark, my beloved knocks. Let me in, my own, my darling, my faultless dove, for my head is drenched with dew, my locks with the damp of night. (Song of Songs 4:1–5:2)

12. To maintain peace between husband and wife: Who is she that comes up from the desert, leaning upon her beloved? Under the apple tree I roused you. It was there your mother conceived you, there she who bore you conceived you. (Song of Songs 8:5)

13. To cure sterility: And if you do obey these rules and observe them carefully, the Lord your God will maintain faithfully for you the covenant that He made an oath with your ancestors.

14. To halt menstrual flow: When she becomes clean of her discharge, she shall count off seven days, and after that she shall be clean. (Leviticus 15:28)

15. For a fever: So Moses cried out to the Lord, saying, "O God, pray heal her." (Numbers 12:13)

16. For consumption: It is a guilt offering. He has incurred guilt before the Lord. (Leviticus 5:19)

17. For success: The Lord was with Joseph, and he was a successful man. He stayed in the house of his Egyptian master. (Genesis 39:2)

18. For profitable trade: Had not the God of my father, the God of Abraham and the fear of Isaac, been with me, you would have sent me away empty-handed. But God took notice of my plight and the toil of my hands, and God gave judgment last night. (Genesis 31:42)

19. On beginning a piece of work: Then all the skilled among those engaged in the work made the tabernacle of ten strips of cloth, which they made of fine twisted linen, blue, purple, and crimson yarns. Into these they worked a design of cherubim. (Exodus 36:8)

20. On entering a new home: On the first day of the first month you shall set up the Tabernacle of the Tent of Meeting. (Exodus 40:2)

21. For safety on a journey: When the Ark was to set out, Moses would say: Advance, O Lord. May your enemies be scattered, and may your foes run from you. And when the Ark halted, he would say: Return, O Lord, you who are Israel's myriads of thousands. (Numbers 10:35–36)

22. To be saved from imminent danger: Therefore say to the Israelite people: I am the Lord. I will free you from the labors of the Egyptians and deliver you from their slavery. And I will take you to be My people, and I will be your God. And you shall know that I, the Lord, am your God who freed you from the labors of the Egyptians. (Exodus 6:6–7)

23. In time of trouble: O my dove, in the cranny of the rocks, hidden by the cliff, let me see your face, let me hear your voice. For your voice is sweet and your face is attractive. (Song of Songs 2:14)

24. To cause an enemy to drown: You made Your wind blow, the sea covered them. They sank like lead in the majestic waters. (Exodus 15:10)

25. To win a war: The Lord, the Warrior—Lord is His name. (Exodus 15:3)

26. To be victorious against robbers: Now the clans of Moab are dismayed, the tribes of Moab, trembling grips them. All the dwellers of Canaan are aghast. (Exodus 15:15)

27. Against slander: In Your great triumph, You break your opponents. You send forth your fury and it consumes them like straw. (Exodus 15:7)

28. To calm a raging river: At the blast of Your nostrils the waters piled up. The floods stood straight like a wall, the deeps froze in the heart of the sea. (Exodus 15:8)

29. To dispel a hallucination: Terror and dread descend upon them. Through the might of your army they are still as stone. Till your people cross over, O Lord, till your people cross over whom You have ransomed. (Exodus 15:16)

30. For intelligence: Lover, indeed of all the people, their hallowed are all in Your hand. They followed in Your steps, accepting Your pronouncements. When Moses charged us with the Teaching as the heritage of the congregation of Jacob. (Deuteronomy 33:3–4)

31. For good health after fasting: Then will I remember My covenant with Jacob. I will also remember My covenant with Isaac, and also My covenant with Abraham, and I will remember the land. (Leviticus 26:42)

33. To bring upon another a curse: No human being who has been proscribed can be ransomed: he shall be put to death. (Leviticus 27:29)

34. Against the evil eye: Then Israel sang this song: Spring up, O well—sing to it. The well which the chieftains dug, which the nobles of the people started, with maces, with their own staffs. And from Midbar to Mattanah, and from Mattanah to Nachaliel, and from Nachaliel to Bamot, and from Bamot to the valley that is in the country of Moab, at the peak of Pisgah overlooking the wasteland. (Numbers 21:17–20)

35. To eradicate evil demons and spirits: You who dwell in the shelter of the Most High and abide in the protection of Shaddai—I say of God, my refuge and stronghold. My God in whom I trust, He will save you from the fowler's trap, from the destructive plague. He will cover you with His pinions, and under His wings you shall take refuge. His truth is a shield and armor. You shall not be afraid of the terror by night nor the arrow that flies by day. Of the pestilence that stalks in darkness, nor of the destruction that ravages at noonday. A thousand may fall at your side, and ten thousand at your right hand. But it shall not come near you. You shall behold only with your eyes, and see the recompense of the wicked. Because you have made the Lord your fortress, and the Most High your refuge, no evil shall befall you, neither shall any plague come near your tent. For God will give His angels charge over you, to guard you in all of your ways. They shall bear you upon their hands, lest you strike your foot against a stone. You shall tread upon the lion and asp, you shall trample on the young lion and serpent. Because he has set his love upon Me, and I will deliver him. I will protect him because he has known My name. He shall call upon Me, and I will answer him. I will be with him in trouble, and rescue him and bring him to honor. I will give him abundance of long life, and he shall witness My salvation. (Psalm 91)

INCANTATIONS

The incantation was another salient element in Jewish magic. An incantation generally refers to a ritual recitation of a charm or spell to produce a magical effect. Most incantations contain the following elements: an appeal to ancient masters of magic, such as a statement that a magical charm was performed by our teacher Moses on behalf of Joshua; the recitation of biblical passages; the invocation of the names of angels; the articulation of holy names; and the mentioning of the actual command. In the Talmud most of the incantations were read in the name of the mother, and this rule of thumb continued into post-Talmudic incantations.

One familiar characteristic of magical incantation is the injunction to do things in reverse, which was believed to be associated with great power when the natural order of things was reversed. This might include saying a verse backward, putting on one's clothing backward, and walking backward.

Another type of incantation to ward off demons is quoted in the Talmud (*Pesachim* 112a), whose power derives from its form. To ward off the evil demon of blindness ("shabriri") we are told that a person should say:

"My mother has told me to beware of shabriri

briri

riri

iri

ri

The idea in this incantation is that as one decreases the letters of the demon shabriri that it begins to shrink, until it finally vanishes.

The mystical word "abracadabra," derived from the Aramaic tongue, was often used as a formula of incantation against fever or inflammation. Medieval patients were advised to wear this magic word, written in the following manner on an amulet, in the belief that it would ward off and cure diseases.

```
A B R A C A D A B R A
A B R A C A D A B R
A B R A C A D A B
A B R A C A D A
A B R A C A D
A B R A C A
A B R A
A B R
A B
A
```

Another charm directed against a fever demon, quoted
from Eleazar of Worms is the following: Ochnotinos,
chnotinos, notinos, otinos, tinos, inos, nos, os.

NUMBERS

For centuries numbers have played an important role in
Jewish folklore. The Talmud *Shabbat* 66b is quoted as
saying that incantations that are not repeated the prescribed
number of times must be said forty-one times. Odd numbers
were always considered lucky, whereas even numbers were
sometimes deemed unlucky. Rabbi Samuel ben Meir, a
Talmudic sage, is quoted as saying that while a fifth cup of
wine might be unnecessary insofar as fear of demons was
concerned, it still might be effective against magic (*Tosefot*,
Talmud *Pesachim* 109b).

Doing things two at a time was considered bad fortune,
and there are many warnings regarding such an action.
These included such instances as two couples marrying on

the same day, marrying off two children at one time, serving as godfather for two brothers, or visiting the same grave twice in one day, just to name a few. In all instances the rationalization against two things at a time seemed to be connected with the rabbinic injunction that two joyous or sacred occasions ought not to be mixed together if it can be helped. Even today, there are rabbis who try not to schedule two Hebrew naming ceremonies for girls on the same day.

The number three is also a popular mystical number, occurring with great frequency in magical texts. Incantations were to be performed either three hours before sunrise or three house before the new moon, or three days in succession. Magical acts often consisted of three stages that required three objects. Incantations were most often to be recited three times and diviners were able to obtain answers to only three questions at one time.

In magic, the number seven was considered the second most popular numeral, next to the number three. Incantations were often repeated seven times for seven consecutive days, seven magical circles were drawn on the ground, and so forth. Demons were said to be notorious for their jealousy of bridegrooms, and the latter were believed to be in grave danger until their brides walk seven times around them (an act that is still performed today in many traditional Jewish wedding ceremonies) under the bridal canopy. Here, the protective power of the circle is used, allowing the practitioner the safety of a protected space from which he can invoke various spirits to carry out his wishes.

Making seven stops at the cemetery before the casket is laid into the ground was said to protect against evil spirits. This act of stopping seven times is still performed in modern times.

Demons had a special proclivity for the number nine.

They were known to assemble in groups of nine in nut trees bearing nine branches. Incantations for their expulsion were to be repeated nine times. If one had seen a demon one was told not to mention its name for nine days, and demonic cures could be accomplished using nine different kinds of herbs.

THE MAGICAL PROCEDURE

Jewish magic generally consisted of a combination of the spoken word that was combined with a symbolic ritual act. The following is a brief summary of the more common magical acts that were known to be performed, especially in medieval Jewish magic.

Expectorating before or after the recitation of the incantation was considered a powerful means of eradicating evil influence (Talmud *Sanhedrin* 101a). Ancients and medievalists all mention the positive values of saliva and spittle. The great medieval physician Moses Maimonides spoke of human saliva of a person who fasts as an especially potent antidote to poison. Today, the expression "pooh pooh pooh" as a refined expectoration can be heard by superstitious persons who use it after witnessing something exceptionally good, such as a beautiful child. It is also done as a prophylaxis so that evil should not happen again.

Interestingly, the New Testament mentions the miraculous powers of the spittle of Jesus: "And they brought to him one that was deaf and stammered . . . and he took him aside from the crowd, and put his fingers into his ears, and touched his tongue with spittle. And looking up to heaven, he sighed and said to him 'Be opened!' . . . and straightaway his tongue was loosed, and he spoke plainly" (Mark 7:32).

The circle is another universal symbol of magic, often used as protection from evil spirits. Perhaps the most renowned miracle worker in the period of the Second Temple is Choni ha-Me'Aggel (i.e., the one who draws circles). This man was known for drawing circles, especially in time of drought. Here is one story to illustrate Choni in action:

> It once happened that the people turned to Choni ha-Me'Aggel and asked him to pray for rain. He prayed, but no rain fell. What did he do? He drew a circle and stood within it and exclaimed, "Master of the Universe, Your children have turned to me because they believe me to be a member of Your household. I swear by Your great name that I will not move from here until You have mercy upon Your children." Rain then began to fall. (Talmud *Taanit* 23a)

Vestiges of the use of the magic circle can still be seen in Jewish rites of passage and life cycle events. In the Orient, for example, the custom is to encircle the coffin seven times while reciting the antidemonic Psalm 91. And as mentioned previously, brides in traditional Jewish marriage ceremonies often encircle their groom seven times with the original intent of warding off the evil demons.

The use of new things for magical procedures was also popular. Thus, for example, when the prophet Elisha was asked by the people of Jericho to purify their water that had been polluted, Elisha said to them, "Bring me a new cruse and put salt inside of it" (II Kings 2:20). Magic circles were to be inscribed with a new sword, new knives were used to engrave spells onto metallic plates, and amulets were to be written on new parchment.

A popular method of transferring the magical spell within one's body was by writing it on foods such as cake or fruit. Thus for example, brides-to-be were often served magic cakes as a sign of good luck. Sometimes magical prescriptions were written on paper, which was then soaked in wine or water and swallowed. At times the magically charged liquid was actually poured onto the body of the person. For instance, one might recite various antidemonic Psalms (such as Psalm 91) over oil and then anoint one's face and hands with it.

SYMPATHETIC MAGIC

Sympathetic magic operates on the principle that acting out an event or imitating the quality of the desired event would facilitate the actual occurrence of the event. Eating honey on Rosh Hashanah, a popular custom even today, was seen as an inducement for a sweet year. Throwing raisins, almonds, rice, and sweet candy at the bridal couple or at a Bar or Bat Mitzvah is very much a kind of magical act, wishing that the couple and child have a sweet and prosperous life.

Births, too, were often facilitated through magic. A woman in labor might be led to and from the threshold of her home and anything that could be opened, such as chests and drawers, was opened. Even the key to the synagogue has its own special power as an opening device useful in facilitating delivery.

Customs associated with death and burial also contain certain aspects of sympathetic magic. For example, one reason for pouring out household water from a house of mourning was that spirits cannot cross water. The intention in this act, therefore, is to ensure that the soul is not trapped inside the home. Graves are not supposed to be left empty overnight, for fear of someone else dying. In the event that a grave was left empty, Russian Jews would often fill it in and bury a rooster inside of it.

Medieval Jewish notions of procreation also contain certain elements of sympathetic magic. Certain food types were believed to influence the "seed" and affect the nature of the offspring. Spicy or heavy foods were said to thicken the blood, thus increasing the flow of semen and produce witty offspring. Salt and salty fish, melons, and vegetables were less conducive to sexual desire and would not produce the same quality offspring that spices, strong wines, and dairy foods produced. What a woman sees when she leaves the *mikveh* prior to her having sexual relations would also influence the child to be conceived. Seeing a dog was said to result in bearing a homely child, whereas seeing a scholar portended of a highly intelligent one.

Sympathetic magic also has a negative side to it. There are many examples of prohibitions designed to ward off the effect of a sympathetic occurrence. For instance, pregnant woman should not step over ropes, for fear that the baby become entangled and perish. Floors ought not to be cleaned or swept after someone leaves the house because this is the customary procedure after someone dies. Nothing should be removed from one's house on Saturday night, because a new week should always begin full. One should not walk backward, because this is the way that the evil walks. Knots were considered negative influences, thus one should be careful to eliminate knots from the hair and from a bridal dress. Perhaps it is for this reason that there is a custom not to bind the Torah scrolls with a knot when it is rolled and closed.

Amulets

A most popular magical device that was either worn by a person or attached to objects or animals was the amulet (*kamea* in Hebrew). Such magical devices have been created and worn by people from earliest times, as humans tried to provide for themselves that extra amount of protection. The custom thus developed for people to have on their persons pieces of paper, parchment, or metal discs inscribed with various formulas that protected the bearer from evil spirits and demons.

It is not known definitively whether amulets were used during biblical times, although it is quite likely that they were. Traditional Judaism does not consider *tefillin* (phylacteries) or the *mezuzah* to be amulets but rather reminders of God's commandments and of the duty of the Jewish people to bear witness to the One God, Sovereign over all.

Amulets are mentioned with frequency in the Talmud. In the Mishneh, amulets are mentioned on two occasions (Talmud *Shabbat* 6:2 and Talmud *Shekalim* 3:2) as being worn for the curative power they were believed to possess.

The Hebrew word *kamea*, meaning amulet, has been said to possibly derive from a root meaning "to bind" or an Arabic root meaning "to hang." The Talmud (*Shabbat* 61b) mentions two kinds of amulets, a written one and one made from the roots of a certain plant. Later amulets were inscribed with quotations relevant to a specific purpose. The text of the Priestly Blessing (Numbers 6:24–26) was considered most effective against the evil eye. This text reads as follows: The Lord bless you and keep you. The Lord make His face to shine on you and be gracious to you. The Lord lift up His countenance and grant you peace.

Combinations of the letters of the many different names of God were frequently used, as were the names of angels. The simplest amulet had an inscription of the name of God (often used were *Yah* or *Shaddai*) on a piece of parchment or metal.

The rabbinic sages in the Talmudic tractate of *Shabbat* 6:2 differentiate between so-called proven amulets and others. Proven ones were able to cure sick people, and persons were permitted to wear these even outside of one's home on the Sabbath. In the Middle Ages, the rabbinic attitude towards amulets varied. Maimonides (also known as Moses ben Maimon or the Rambam) strongly opposed the use of amulets, and came out strongly against them in his *Guide to the Perplexed* (1:61). On the other hand, Nachmanides (also known as Moses ben Nachman or the Ramban) permitted the use of them.

Many mystical kabbalistic texts, including *Sefer Yetzirah* and *Sefer Raziel* contain instructions for the preparation of amulets and other charms. Three biblical verses (Exodus 14:19–21) were believed to have the highest mystical significance, because each of them consists of seventy-two letters, corresponding to the seventy-two letters of one of the mysterious names of God. Hence, these verses were assumed to represent the ineffable divine name, and they were inserted in the amulets in varied forms as an appeal to God for protection.

EXAMPLES OF AMULETS

The following is a brief summary of the variety of amulets that are found and often still used today in Jewish tradition:

Magic Triangle

By gradually reducing the size of an inscription, the evil spirit is eased out of its victim and its potency is substantially diminished.

Squares and Rectangles

These are divided into boxes, each of which contains one or more Hebrew letters. Thus, acrostics can be formed in which powerful inscriptions may be secretly placed in the amulets. The squares vary from those of nine boxes to those of 64 or even 100 boxes. In the illustration of the magic square, the initial Hebrew letters of Deuteronomy 7:15 (And God will take away from you all sickness, and God will put none of the evil diseases of Egypt which you know upon you, but will lay them upon all of those that hate you) are used as a protection against illness.

ב	פ	ו	ח	כ	מ	י	ו
ו	ב	פ	ו	ח	כ	מ	י
י	ו	ב	פ	ו	ח	כ	מ
מ	י	ו	ב	פ	ו	ח	כ
כ	מ	י	ו	ב	פ	ו	ח
ח	ב	מ	י	ו	ב	פ	ו
ו	ח	כ	מ	י	ו	ב	פ
פ	ו	ח	כ	מ	י	ו	ב

Figure 1:1. Magical square, with initial letters of Deuteronomy 7:15 used as a protection against illness.

Hexagram

The Star of David, consisting of six points, often contains the Hebrew letters for Jerusalem (*yerushalayim*) or King David (*melech David*). The hexagram symbol also is known to appear in written amulets.

The Menorah

The seven branched candlestick is often found on the so-called *shiviti* amulets from Persia. *Shiviti* is the opening Hebrew word of the verse in Psalm 16:8 "I have set the Lord always before me." In the silver amulets only the initial Hebrew letters of the words are used but in the parchment ones the verses are written out in full. Tradition says that King David's shield was shaped like these silver amulets, and headed with the words "I have set the Lord always before me."

The Hand

From the Arabic word for five, this amulet looks like a hand, often containing the evil eye in the center.

GEMS

Precious stones and gems have also been used for magical purposes, known to ward off evil spirits and demons. The Bible (Exodus 28:17–20) speaks of the twelve gems engraved with the tribal names, known as the *Urim* and *Thummim*, which were attached to the breastplate of the high priest. Used as a sacred means of divination, the gems were known for their ability to answer questions on occasions fateful for the Israelite nation.

The following is a summary of several gemes that are discussed in the unpublished fourteenth-century manuscript called *Sefer Gematriot*:

1. Odem (Ruby): Connecting with Reuben, this stone was used to prevent the woman who wears it from suffering a miscarriage.

2. Pitdah (Topaz): The stone of Simeon, its use includes that of chilling the body in addition to being useful in affairs of the heart.

3. Bareket (Emerald): This is the stone of evil, making a person wise and helping to light up his eyes.

4. Nofech (Carbuncle): This green stone, the stone of Judah, functions to add strength to a person and help that person become victorious in battle.

5. Sapir (Sapphire): The stone of Issachar, it is purple-blue in color and is known for its outstanding ability to cure ailments.

6. Yahalom (Emerald): This is the stone of Zebulun, able to bring a person success in trade. It is also known for its ability to bring a person sleep.

7. Leshem (Jacinth): The stone of Dan, it allows the face of man to be seen in it.

8. Shebo (Agate): This is the stone of Naphtali, helping to prevent a person from stumbling or falling.

9. Achlamah (Amethyst): The stone of Gad, it is useful in war.

10. Tarshish (Beryl): The stone of Ashur, it is useful for burning up bad food in one's body.

11. Shoham (Onyx): This is Joseph's stone, bestowing grace upon the bearer and assisting in getting people to listen to the bearer's words.

12. Yashfeh (Jasper): The stone of Benjamin, it has the power to restrain both one's tongue and one's blood.

MAGIC, MEDICINE, AND HEALING

Much of ancient medicine consisted of a combination of science, superstition and folklore. Supernatural agencies were often considered as causes of illness and disease, and remedies often included incantations accompanied by other rites and rituals. The following are some rabbinic passages which reflect the many recipes that belong to the category of folk medicine.

1. Remedy for a fever: Abaye said: My mother told me that for a daily fever one should take a new *zuz* coin, go to a salt deposit, take the *zuz*'s weight in salt, and tie the salt inside the collar of his shirt with a band of twined strands of wool. If this remedy does not help, the patient should sit at a crossroads, and when he sees a large ant carrying something, he should take it, put it into a brass tube, close the tube's openings with lead, and seal it with sixty seals. He should then shake it, lift it on his back, and say to it, "Your burden be upon me, and my burden be upon you." If this remedy does not help, he should take a new jar, small in

size, go to the river, and say to it, "River, O river, lend me
a jarful of water for a guest who happens to be visiting me."
He should circle the jar seven times about his head, then
pour its water behind his back and say to it, "River, O river,
take back the water you gave me, for the guest who visited
me came for a day and left the same day." (Talmud *Shabbat*
66b)

2. Remedy for tertian fever: Rabbi Huna said: As a
remedy for tertian fever, one should procure seven prickles
from seven date palms, seven chips from seven beams,
seven pegs from seven bridges, seven handfuls of ash from
seven ovens, seven pinches of earth from seven graves,
seven bits of pitch from seven ships, seven seeds of cumin,
and seven hairs from the beard of an old dog, and tie them
inside the collar of his shirt with a band of twined strands of
wool. (Talmud *Shabbat* 67a)

3. Remedy for fever accompanied by shivering: Rabbi
Yochanan said: For fever accompanied by shivering, one
should take a knife made entirely of iron, go to a place
where there is a thornbush, and tie to it bands of twined
strands of wool. On the first day, he should make a slight
notch in the bush and say, "The angel of the Lord appeared
unto him . . . And Moses said: . . . I will turn aside
now . . . and see why the bush is not burnt." [Exodus
3:2–3]
On the following day, he should make another small
notch and say, "When the Lord saw that he turned aside to
see" [Exodus 3:4]. The next day, he should make a third
small notch and say, "Do not draw near" [Exodus 3:5]. And
when the fever has stopped, he should bend the bush and
then cut it down as he says, "Thornbush, O thornbush, not

because you are higher than all other trees in the field did the Holy One have His Presence abide upon you, but He had His Presence abide upon you because you are lower than all other trees in the field. And even as the fire fled Chananiah, Mishael, and Azariah when it saw them, so may the fire that sees so-and-so son of so-and-so flee from him." (Talmud *Shabbat* 67a)

4. Remedy for a rash: For a rash, one should say, "Bazbaziah, Masmasiah, Kaskasiah, Sharlai, and Amarlai"— these are the angels who were sent out from the land of Sodom to heal those smitten with a rash—"Bazakh, Bazikh, Bazbazikh, Masmassikh, Kammon, Kamikh, your color is to remain what it is now, your color is to remain what it is now. Your place is to be confined to where it is now. Your place is to be confined to where it is now. Like one whose seed is locked up, or like a mule that is not fruitful and cannot increase, so may your seed not be fruitful nor increase in the body of so-and-so son of so-and-so (Talmud *Shabbat* 67a)

5. Remedy for epilepsy: Against epilepsy, one should say, "A sword drawn, a sling stretched, its name is not Yukhav—'sickness and pain.'" (Talmud *Shabbat* 67a)

6. Remedy for depression: If a person is seized by depression, what is the way to heal him? Red meat broiled over coals, and diluted wine. (Talmud *Gittin* 67b)

7. Remedy for a fever: Abbaye said: My mother told me that the remedy for a fever on the first day is to drink a small pitcher of water. If the fever persists for two days, to let blood; if three days, to eat red meat broiled over coals and drink diluted wine. For continuing fever, a person should get a black hen, tear it lengthwise and crosswise, shave the middle of his head, put the hen on his head, and leave it there till it sticks fast. Then he should go down to the river, stand in the water up to his neck until he is faint, and then he should take a dip and come up.

For fever, one should eat red meat broiled over coals and diluted wine. For a chill, one should eat fat meat broiled over coals and drink undiluted wine. (Talmud *Gittin* 67b)

8. Remedy for blood rushing to one's head: For blood rushing to the head, one should take bark of a box tree, a willow, and myrtle, an olive tree, a sea willow, and a cynodon, and boil them together. Then one should pour three hundred cups [of the concoction] on one side of his head and three hundred cups on the other side. If this remedy does not help, one should take white roses all of whose leaves are on one side of the stem, boil them, and pour sixty cups of the boiled roses on one side of his head and sixty cups on the other side of his head. (Talmud *Gittin* 68b)

9. Remedy for a migraine headache: For a migraine, one should take a woodcock and cut its throat with a white silver coin over the side of the head where the pain is concentrated, taking care that the blood does not blind his eyes. Then he should hang the bird on his doorpost, so that he can rub against it when he comes in and when he exits. (Talmud *Gittin* 69a)

10. Remedy for cataracts: For a cataract, one should take a seven-hued scorpion, dry it out in the shade, and mix two parts of ground kohl to one part of ground scorpion;

then, with a paintbrush, apply three drops to each eye—no more, lest the eye burst. (Talmud *Gittin* 69a)

11. Remedy for night and day blindness: For night blindness, a person should take a rope made of wool and with it tie one of his own legs to the leg of a dog, and children should rattle potsherds behind him, saying, "Old dog, stupid cock." He should collect seven pieces of raw meat from seven houses, place them in a door socket, and then have the dog eat them over the ash pit of the town. After that, he should untie the rope, and people should say to him, "Blindness of so-and-so son of so-and-so, let go of so-and-so son of so-and-so, and instead seize the pupils of the dog's eyes."

For day blindness, a person should take seven milts from the insides of animals and roast them over a blood letter's shard. While the blind man sits inside the house, another man should sit outside, and the blind man should say to him, "Give me something to eat." The sighted man should then reply, "Take and eat." After the blind man has eaten, he should then break the shard. Otherwise, the blindness will come back. (Talmud *Gittin* 69a)

12. Remedy to stop a nosebleed: To stop a nosebleed, a man should call a priest whose name is Levi and write "Levi" backward, or else call any other man and write backward, "I am Papi Shila bar Sumki," or else write "the taste of the bucket in water of blemish."

If this remedy does not work, one should take clover roots, the rope of an old bed, papyrus, saffron, and the red part of a palm branch, and burn them all together. Then he should take a fleece of wool, twine it into wicks, steep those in vinegar, roll them in ashes, and put them into his nostrils.

If this remedy does not help, he should look for a water channel running from east to west, stand aside it, pick up some clay with his right hand from under his left foot and with his left hand from under his right foot, twine two more fleeces of wool into wicks, rub these in clay and put them into his nostrils. If this remedy does not help either, he should sit under a drainpipe and have people bring water, and sprinkle it over him as they say, "Even as these waters will stop, so shall the blood of so-and-so son of so-and-so stop." (Talmud *Gittin* 69a)

13. Remedy to stop bleeding from the mouth: To stop bleeding from the mouth, the blood should be tested by means of a wheaten straw. If the straw is softened, the blood comes from the lung and there is a remedy for that. If the straw is not softened, the blood comes from the liver, and there is no remedy for that.

If the blood comes from the lung, what is the remedy? He should take seven fistfuls of jujube berry, three fistfuls of lentils, a fistful of cumin, a fistful of string, and a quantity equal to all these of the ileum of a firstborn animal. Then he should cook the mixture and eat it, washing it down with strong beer made during the month of Tevet. (Talmud *Gittin* 69a)

14. Remedy for a toothache: For a toothache, Rabbah bar R. Chuna said: A man should take a whole head of garlic, grind it with oil and salt and apply it on his thumbnail to the side where the tooth aches. He must put a rim of dough around it, thus taking care that it does not touch his flesh, as it may cause leprosy. (Talmud *Gittin* 69a)

15. Remedy for catarrh in the head: For a catarrh in the head, one should take gum ammoniac equal to the size of a pistachio nut, galbanun equal to the size of a walnut, honey cake, a spoonful of white honey, and a Mahozan *natla* (i.e., a small vessel) of clear wine, and boil them together. When the gum ammoniac comes to a boil, all the others have boiled enough. If this remedy does not help, he should take a quarter of a *log* of milk of white goats, let it drip on three stalks of cabbage, and stir it with a stem of marjoram. When that stem comes to a boil, all the others have boiled enough. If even this remedy does not help, he should take the excrement of a white dog and knead it with balsam. If he can possibly avoid it, he should not resort to eating the dog's excrement, as it disintegrates the limbs. (Talmud *Gittin* 69a–b)

16. Remedy for swelling of the spleen: For swelling of the spleen, a man should take seven water leeches and dry them in the shade, and every day drink two or three in wine. If this does not help, he should take the spleen of a she-goat that has not yet had young, put it inside an oven, stand by it, and say, "As this spleen has dried up, so may the spleen of so-and-so son of so-and-so dry up." If this remedy does not help, he should look for the corpse of a person who died on the Sabbath, take the corpse's hand, put it against his own spleen and say, "As the hand of this one has dried up, so may the spleen of so-and-so son of so-and-so dry up." (Talmud *Gittin* 69b)

17. Remedy to restore virility: Abbaye said: One who is unsure of his virility should bring three small measures of thorny saffron, pound it, boil it in wine, and drink it. Rabbi Yochanan said, "This is exactly what restored me to the vigor of my youth." (Talmud *Gittin* 70a)

18. To restore strength to the heart: Abbaye said: My mother told me: One who suffers from weakness of the heart should get meat from the right leg of a ram and dried cattle excrement dropped during the month of Nisan. If one has no dried cattle droppings, one should get chips of willow and roast the meat over them. One should then eat it and then drink diluted wine. (Talmud *Eruvin* 29b)

19. Remedy for a scorpion bite: Abbaye said: My mother told me: A six-year-old child stung on his birthday by a scorpion is not likely to live. What is a remedy? The gall of a white stork in beer. This is to be rubbed into the wound, and the rest should be given to the child to drink. A one-year-old stung on his birthday by a wasp is also not likely to live. What is a remedy? The bast of a date palm in water. This should be rubbed into the wound, and the rest should be given to the child to drink. (Talmud *Ketubot* 50a)

20. Remedy for a wound to the body: Samuel said: A wound is to be regarded as so dangerous that the Sabbath may be profaned for it. What is the remedy? To stop the bleeding, pepperwort in vinegar; to induce new growth of flesh, peelings of cynodon and the paring of a thornbush, or worms from a dunghill. (Talmud *Avodah Zarah* 28a)

21. Remedy for a growth on the eye: Rabbi Safra said: A berry-sized growth on the eye is an emissary of the angel of death. What is the remedy? Rue in honey or parsley in an inferior wine. In the meantime, a berry resembling it in size should be brought and rolled over it. A white berry for a white growth, and a black berry for a black growth. (Talmud *Avodah Zarah* 28a)

22. Remedy for a bacterial infection: Rava said: A bacterial infection is a forerunner of a fever. What is the remedy? It should be spanned sixty times with the middle finger and then cut open crosswise and lengthwise. This should be done only if its head is not white. If its head is white, it is not dangerous. (Talmud *Avodah Zarah* 28a)

23. Remedy for a fissure in the rectum: When Rabbi Jacob was suffering from a fissure in the rectum, Rabbi Ammi (some say Rabbi Assi) directed him to take seven grains from the purple alkali plant, wrap them in a shirt collar, tie around it a white wool thread, dip the poultice in white naphtha, burn it, and powder the fissure with the ashes. While preparing the poultice, he was to take kernels of the nut of a thornbush and apply their split to the fissure. This should be done if the fissure is external. What should be done if it is internal? One should take some fat of a she-goat that has borne no young, melt it, and apply it within the anus. If this remedy does not help, one should take three melon leaves that have been dried in the shade, burn them, and powder the fissure with the ashes. If this remedy does not help, one should apply olive oil mixed with wax and cover the fissure with strips of linen in summer and cotton wool in winter. (Talmud *Avodah Zarah* 28a–b)

24. Remedy for an earache: Rabbi Abbahu had an earache. So Rabbi Yochanan (some say the sages in the house of study) instructed him: He should take the kidney of a hairless goat, cut it crosswise and lengthwise, put it over glowing coals, and pour the water that comes out of it—neither hot nor cold, but tepid—into the ear. If this remedy does not work, he should take the fat of a large scarab beetle, melt it, and let it drip into the ear. If this remedy does not work, the ear should be filled with oil. Then seven wicks should be made out of clover stocks, with a garlic stem and a woolen tassel attached to one end of each wick, and the wick set alight. The other end is placed inside the ear. The ear should be exposed to the fire, but care must be taken that there be no wind. Each wick should be replaced by another when it is used up. If this remedy does not work, he should take two of the danda plant that has not been combed and place it within the ear, and place the ear near the fire. Care should be taken that there be no wind. If this remedy does not work, he should take the hundred-year-old tube of an old can, fill it with rock salt, then burn it and apply the ashes to the sore part of the ear. (Talmud *Avodah Zarah* 28b)

25. Remedy for scurvy: When Rabbi Yochanan suffered from scurvy, he went to a Roman noblewoman who prepared something for him on Thursday and Friday. What did she prepare for him? Rabbi Acha son of Rabbi Ammi said: The water of leaven, olive oil, and salt. Rabbi Yemar said: Leaven itself, olive oil, and salt. Rabbi Ashi said: The fat of a goose together with its wing. Abbaye said: I tried all of these without effecting a cure for myself, until an Arab recommended: "Take the pits of olives that have not grown to one-third of their size, burn them in fire on a new rake, and stick them to the inside of the gums." I did so and was cured. (Talmud *Yoma* 84a)

26. Remedy for jaundice: One inflicted by jaundice should be fed the flesh of a donkey. One bitten by a mad dog should be fed the lobe of its liver. So said Rabbi Matia ben Heresh. But the sages said: There is no healing whatever in such remedies. (Talmud *Yoma* 84a)

27. Remedy for worms in the bowels: As a remedy for worms in the bowels, pennyroyal should be eaten. With what should it be eaten? With seven black dates. What causes worms in the bowels? Raw meat and water on an empty stomach, fat meat on an empty stomach, ox meat on an empty stomach, nuts on an empty stomach, or shoots of fenugreek eaten on an empty stomach and washed down with water. If there are no black dates, one should swallow with white cress. If that does not help, he should fast, then fetch some fat meat, put it over glowing coals, suck out the marrow from a bone, and gulp down vinegar. Not vinegar, others say, because it affects the liver. If that does not help, he should obtain the scrapings of a thornbush that was scraped from top to bottom—not from the bottom to the top, lest the worms issue through his mouth—and boil the scrapings in beer at twilight. The next day, he should hold his nose and make himself drink it. When he relieves himself, he should do so on the stripped parts of a date palm. (Talmud *Shabbat* 109b)

28. Remedy for drinking uncovered water: As an antidote for drinking uncovered water, one should drink juice of the shepherd's flute plant. If that does not work, one should get five roses and five cups of beer, boil them together until the brew reduces to an *anpak* (i.e., unit of liquid measure), and drink it. The mother of Rabbi Ahadboi bar Amni prepared a portion of one rose and one cup of beer for a certain man. She brought the mix to a boil and made him drink it. Then she lit the oven, swept it out to cool it, placed a brick on it, and had him sit on it to perspire, and the poison of the snake's venom oozed out of him in a liquid that was the color of a green leaf palm. Rabbi Ivia suggested as a remedy for uncovered water the following: a fourth of a *log* (i.e., unit of liquid measure) of milk from a white goat. Rabbi Huna bar Judah said: He should obtain a sweet etrog, scoop it out, fill it with honey, set it over burning embers to boil, and then eat it. Rabbi Haninah said: One should drink some urine forty days old as a remedy: a *barazina* (i.e., unit of liquid measure) of it for a wasp sting; a fourth of a *log* for a scorpion's sting; and a half of a *log* for uncovered water. A *log* of urine is effective even against witchcraft. (Talmud *Shabbat* 109b)

29. Remedy for swallowing a baby snake: One who swallows a baby snake should eat cuscuta with salt and run three *mil*. Rabbi Shimi bar Ashi saw a man swallow a baby snake. He appeared to the man in the guise of a horseman and made him eat cuscuta with salt and run three *mil* before him, and the snake issued from the man rib by rib.

He who is bitten by a snake should obtain the embryo of a white she-ass, tear it open, and put it over him, provided, however, that the ass was not found to be suffering from a serious organic disease.

A certain officer of Pumbedita was once bitten by a snake. Now, there were thirteen white she-asses in Pumbedita. All were torn open, and each was found to be suffering from a serious organic disease. There was another she-ass on the outskirts of the city, but before they could go and bring it, a lion devoured it. Then Abbaye suggested, "Perhaps he was bitten by the snake of the sages, for which there is no cure." The people replied, "This is so, our master, for when Rav died, Rabbi Isaac bar Bisna decreed that in token of mourning, myrtles and palm branches should not be brought to a wedding feast to the sound of bells, yet this officer did go and bring myrtles and palm branches to a wedding feast to the sound of bells." So a snake bit him, and he died.

If a snake winds itself around a person, that one should wade into water, put a basket over his head, and dislodge the snake. When the snake climbs up to the basket, he should shove the basket onto the water, go up out of the water, and get away quickly.

When a man is scented by a snake, if he has a companion with him, he should ride upon the companion's shoulders a distance of four cubits. If he has no companion, he should jump over a ditch full of water. If there is no ditch, he should ford a river. And at night he should place his bed on four casks and sleep out of doors under the vault of heaven. He should also bring four she-cats and tie them to the four legs of the bed, then scatter chips of wood all around, so that when the cats hear the sound of the snake coming over the chips, they will devour it.

He who is chased by a snake should run toward sandy places. (Talmud *Shabbat* 109b–110a)

30. Remedy for a stuck meat bone in one's throat: He who has a meat bone stuck in his throat should bring more of that kind of meat, place it on his head, and say, "One by one, go down, swallow; swallow, go down, one by one." If it is a fish bone, he should say, "You are stuck like a pin, locked up as in a cuirass. Go down, go down." (Talmud *Shabbat* 67a)

31. Remedy for bad breath: It was said in the name of Rabbi Chiyya: After every food eat salt and after every beverage drink water and you will come to no harm. [One who does not do this] by day, he is liable to be troubled with an evil-smelling mouth. (Talmud *Berachot* 40a)

32. Remedy for foot trouble: There was a person who suffered with his feet and went around to all the doctors and

could not find a cure until at last one came and said to him:
If you want to be cured, there is a very easy way of doing
it: plaster your feet with excrement of cattle. (Song of Songs
Rabbah, II, 3, 2)

33. Remedy for heartburn: Rabbi Chama ben Haninah
said: One who takes regularly black cumin will not suffer
heartburn. (Talmud *Berachot* 40a)

SUPERSTITION

Laws and customs are the building blocks of Jewish life, unifying the community. Whereas a law derives from the Torah and the Talmud, custom derives from popular practice. It is created by the people, serving the needs of the general community. This is why each community generally has developed its own peculiar customs.

Each community over time also has developed its own peculiar folklore and practices that are associated with it. Folklore refers to the creative, spiritual, and cultural practices and teachings of a people that are handed down, mainly by oral tradition, from generation to generation. It might include popular tales, legends, songs, and anecdotes that are transmitted primarily by word of mouth.

Within folklore one will also find a variety of superstitions. A superstition is generally defined as any custom or act that is based on an irrational fear rather than on tradition, belief, reason, or knowledge. America is filled with superstitious beliefs, such as the unluckiness of a Friday that happens to fall on the thirteenth of a given month. Walking under a ladder is considered bad luck by many in Western culture. Judaism, too, is filled with a variety of superstitious beliefs. Even for contemporary Jews, superstition and folklore are foundations of warm sentimental waters, evoking memories of parents and grandparents who often warned us of things not to do and things to avoid. As silly as many of these sounded, they were done with the goal of safeguarding a person from danger and the evil that was lurking in the air.

This chapter summarizes a cross-section of Judaism's superstitions, many of which continue to play an important role in the life of a contemporary Jew.

SUPERSTITIONS RELATED TO CIRCUMCISION

1. Red ribbons and garlic were placed on a baby's crib to ward off evil spirits.

2. A knife was placed under the pillow of the mother the night before the circumcision to protect her from evil spirits.

3. During a difficult labor, a Torah belt was placed around the belly of the mother.

4. Candy was often placed under the bed of the mother to draw the attention of the evil spirits away from her and the baby.

5. During the Middle Ages there arose a custom of "cradling" the baby boy after his circumcision. In this ceremony a copy of the Five Books of Moses was placed upon him in his cradle, and the people standing about him said, "May this child fulfill what is written in this book!"

6. In Eastern Europe it was customary to throw sugar, raisins, cake, and coins into the baby's cradle before the child was placed in it, as an omen for a sweet and abundant life.

SUPERSTITIONS RELATED TO NAMING A CHILD

1. In early times it was the custom to name a child immediately upon birth. Later, the name was postponed because it was feared that the name presented a "handle" with which the baby could be reached by the Angel of Death. It was thought that by postponing the naming, the Angel of Death could not reach the child during the most fragile first days of life.

2. In the Middle Ages some Jews had secret names that they would not reveal to anyone.

3. Some Jews follow the custom of refusing to marry a person who has the same name as their mother or father. This custom arose from fear that the Angel of Death might confuse two persons with the same name, leading to the premature death of one or the other.

4. In Eastern Europe children would sometimes be given additional names that symbolized length of years, such as the Yiddish name *alter*, meaning old person. Giving a child such a name was believed to increase the child's longevity.

5. A custom that is still seen today is to change the name of a person who is extremely ill and near death. Accordingly, such a person might be given the new name of *Chayim* ("life" for a male) or *Chaya* ("living being" for a female) in order to deceive the angel of death through this change in identity.

6. It is an Ashkenazic custom not to name a child after a living person. Confronted with two children of the same name, it was believed that the evil spirits are likely as not to choose the wrong one upon whom to lavish their unwelcome attentions.

7. People would often try to avoid entering the home of a sick person who bore their name, for fear that the evil spirit and Angel of Death might confuse them for the person who was ill.

SUPERSTITIONS AND WEDDINGS

1. It was believed that demons and evil spirits are notorious for their jealousy of bridegrooms and the latter were believed to be in grave danger until their brides walk seven times around them under the bridal canopy. Here we see the protective power of the circle, frequently used as we have seen in magical practice.

2. Fifteenth-century bridegrooms were described as wearing mourning garb and spreading ashes upon themselves in order to fool the evil forces.

3. The bride often carried a lighted torch or candle as a way of warding off evil spirits.

4. The noise from the breaking of the glass at the end of every Jewish marriage ceremony was said to be a protective measure against the forces of evil spirits and demons.

5. The custom of the fast of the bride and bridegroom on the day of their wedding has been known to fool the evil spirits into thinking that it is a day of mourning rather than one of ultimate joy.

6. Breaking a dish when announcing the engagement of a Jewish couple is said to frighten away evil spirits.

7. Getting married on a Tuesday is thought to be an auspicious day for a wedding because in the biblical creation story in the Book of Genesis God twice says on the third day that "it was good." On all of the other days of creation the phrase "it was good" is mentioned only one time.

SUPERSTITIONS AND DEATH

1. Making seven stops before the casket is laid into the ground at a cemetery was said to protect against the evil eye.

2. Pouring out household water from the house of a mourner is done so that the evil spirits could not cross the water. The intention was to ensure that the soul did not remain trapped inside the house.

3. Watching and caring for a deceased corpse (before burial) while reading various Psalms was considered a strong antidote to evil spirits.

4. Some people follow the custom after leaving a cemetery of plucking blades of grass and throwing them behind one's back, thus repelling the evil spirits that lurk behind.

OTHER JEWISH SUPERSTITIONS

1. Demons like whistling. Therefore, the prohibition of whistling in one's house was a superstitious way of making one's home less attractive to demons. (This custom is traceable to the Kiev area of Russia during the early nineteenth century.)

2. Chewing on thread if one is wearing a garment upon which someone is actively sewing is a superstition often followed today. Some have based this folkloristic custom as related to the remains of the deceased being sewn into their burial shrouds. As an avoidance of this, some people choose not to sew onto garments that they are wearing. The act of chewing thread shows that the individual is very much alive and in this world!

3. Expectorating and using one's saliva was an ancient way of repelling evil spirits. Today, saying the phrase "pooh pooh pooh" after witnessing something wonderful or beautiful such as a newborn baby was considered an antidote to evil.

4. When a Jewish person today travels to a foreign country, especially to the State of Israel, that person is often given money by his or her friends, which he in turn is asked to give to charity. According to Talmudic legend, one will be protected from harm if one is involved in the commission of performing a *mitzvah*.

5. Not counting Jewish people is a superstitious custom. In the Bible, counting was often connected to taking the census for purposes of a war of aggression. Some considered the prohibition of counting people as a means of foiling the Angel of Death. Today, in order to determine whether the proper number of persons (i.e., ten) are present for a quorum (i.e., *minyan*), several ten-word liturgical sentences are used, with each word meant to correspond to one person. One such Hebrew phrase is the following: *"Hosheeya et amecha uvarech et nachalatecha uraym venasym ad ha' olam"* (Bless and deliver Your people, Your heritage, sustain them forever).

6. Closing books that are left open is still a superstitious practice that is seen in synagogues today. The practice likely relates to the ancient belief that an open book can be more easily inhabited by an evil spirit who can work to distort its meaning.

7. No walking on thresholds was a superstitious Jew's way of avoiding evil demons that were said to reside within the threshold itself.

8. Salt was considered an antidote to evil spirits. Placing salt in one's home or in one's pocket was a way of eradicating them.

9. Metal was believed to posses protective powers. That is why some Jewish people today like to wear or carry safety pins with them, which have the power to repel evil spirits.

10. Three things take away a person's eyesight: combing one's head while the hair is dry, drinking the drippings of wine, and putting on shoes while one's feet are still wet. (Talmud *Pesachim* 111b)

11. Food suspended from the ceiling in a house was said to bring on poverty. Other actions that could bring on poverty included bran and crumbs in a house, a bowl covering the spout of a jug, and drinking water out of a bowl. (Talmud *Pesachim* 111b)

12. The following cause a person to live in fear: eating cress without washing one's hands, trimming hair without washing one's hands, and paring nails without washing one's hands. Putting a finger in one's nostrils is a step to fear. (Talmud *Pesachim* 112a)

13. Food and drink that are kept under a bed will have a tormenting spirit rest on them. (Talmud *Pesachim* 112a)

14. A person must not drink water either on the night ushering in a Wednesday or the night ushering in the Sabbath, and if he does drink, his blood is on his own head because of the danger of an evil spirit. Similarly, a person should not drink water from rivers or pools at night, and if he drinks, his blood is on his own head because of the danger. (Talmud *Pesachim* 112a)

15. If a person is frightened, even though he sees nothing, it is because his planet sees it. The remedy is to recite the *Shema*. (Talmud Megillah 3a)

16. Five things make a person forget his learning: eating something of which a mouse or a cat has eaten, eating the heart of a beast, frequent consumption of olives, drinking waste bathwater, and washing one's feet one foot above the other. Some say that one who puts his clothes under his pillow forgets his learning. (Talmud *Horayot* 3b)

17. Five things improve one's learning: eating wheat bread and wheat itself, eating a roasted egg without salt, frequent consumption of olive oil, frequent indulgence in wine and spices, and drinking the water that is left from kneading dough. Some say also dipping one's finger into salt and licking it. (Talmud *Horayot* 13b)

18. Although olives cause one to forget seventy years of study, olive oil restores seventy years of study. (Talmud *Horayot* 13b)

19. Ten things adversely affect one's capacity to learn: passing under a camel's bit and under the camel itself, passing between two camels, passing between two women, a woman passing through two men, passing within smelling distance of a decaying carcass, passing under a bridge beneath which no water has flowed for forty days, eating bread insufficiently baked, eating meat out of a soup ladle, drinking from a water channel that runs through the graveyard, and looking in the face of a dead body. Others say that one who reads the inscription on a grave is also subject to the same disability. (Talmud *Horayot* 13b)

20. One who takes sick should not speak of it the first day, lest his luck turn worse. After the first day, he may speak freely of his illness. (Talmud *Berachot* 55b)

DEMONS, SPIRITS, AND EVIL FORCES

Defending against evil spirits and demons was a concern of all people in the Ancient Near East. Considered messengers of the lord of the underworld, demons (in Hebrew, *mazzikim*) were believed to live in the wilderness and near graves. Many of them were spirits of the dead, especially of persons who died a violent death and were not properly laid to rest. Sometimes even sickness was thought to be caused by demonic possession.

Amulets and a variety of incantations were composed with the intention of warding off evil spirits and demons. In one seventh-century Phoenician amulet we find the following incantation intended to protect a woman in childbirth: "Incantations: O Flying One, O goddess, O Sasam . . . O god, O Strangler of Lambs. The house I enter you shall not enter; the court I rend you shall not tread . . ."

Surrounded by animistic notions of primitive people, the Jews absorbed some of these and developed a variety of legends of their own concerning evil spirits that wield a destructive power over human beings.

DEMONS IN THE BIBLE

In the Book of Samuel I, 16:14–16, we learn firsthand of evil spirits that come to trouble the mind of King Saul:

> Now the spirit of God departed from Saul, and an evil spirit from God terrified him. And Saul's servants said to him: "Behold now, an evil spirit from God terrifies you. Let our lord now command your servants that are before you, to seek out a man who is skilled on the harp. And it shall be, when the evil spirit from God comes to you, that he shall play with his hand, and you will be cured . . ."

This story concludes when David plays the harp for Saul, who finds soothing relief in the music and the evil spirits depart from his body. What is important to remember in this story is that the evil spirits do not possess an independent will, but rather are sent by God and are fully under God's control and Will.

DEMONS IN THE TALMUD AND MIDRASH

There are a number of references in the form of legend related to demons, both in the Talmud and midrashic sources. Here is a sampling of them.

1. This rabbinic statement identifies the time of day when demons are created: Demons were created at twilight on the eve of the first Sabbath. (Based on Ethics of the Fathers, 5:6)

2. In the following midrash we learn that semen that is discharged for purposes other than procreation is said to be utilized by evil spirits to produce their own kind:

Rabbi Jeremiah ben Eleazar said: In all of the years that Adam was under the ban [because he ate of the forbidden fruit], he begot evil spirits—both male and female demons. For it is written, "Adam lived a hundred and thirty years, and begot a son in his own likeness, after his own image" [Genesis 5:3], from which it follows that until that time he did not beget after his own image. (Talmud *Eruvin* 18b)

3. This midrash describes some of the physical characteristics of demons:

Our rabbis taught: Six things are said concerning demons. With regard to three, they are like ministering angels. With regard to three others, they are like human beings. They are like ministering angels in that they have wings, they fly from one end of the world to the other, and they can hear what goes on behind the curtain of heaven. They are like human beings in that they eat and drink like humans, they procreate like humans and they die like human beings. (Talmud *Chagigah* 16a)

4. The midrash instructs a person who wishes to become aware of the existence of demons:

One who desires to become aware of demons' existence should take carefully sifted ashes and sprinkle
them in his bed. In the morning, he will notice
something like the tracks of a cock. One who wishes to
see them should take the afterbirth of a black cat that is
the offering of a black cat and a firstborn of a firstborn.
One should parch the afterbirth in fire, grind it into
powder, and put a generous pinch of the mixture into
his eyes. Then one will see the demons. (Talmud
Berachot 6a)

5. This statement describes the demon of bitter destruction:

Rabbi Huna said in the name of Rabbi Yose: The
demon bitter destruction is covered with scales and
hair and shines with his one eye. That eye is in the
middle of his chest. He is powerless when it is cool in
the shade and hot in the sun, but only when it is hot in
both shade and sun. He rolls like a ball and from the
seventeenth of Tammuz until the ninth of Av, he has
power after ten o'clock in the morning and until three
o'clock in the afternoon. Any person who sees this
demon falls on his face and dies. (Midrash, Numbers
Rabbah 12:3)

6. The following rabbinic tale tells of the efficacy of
prayer in working to eradicate a demon:

It once occurred that a certain demon haunted Abaye's
house of study. Even though during the day people
entered into prayers, they still were harmed. Abaye
then said to his students: "Let no one offer lodging to

Rabbi Acha [so that he would be forced to spend the night in Abaye's house of study]. Perhaps through his merit a miracle will take place."

Rabbi Acha went to the house of study where he did spend the night. The demon appeared to him as a seven-headed dragon. Each time, Rabbi Acha fell to his knees in prayer, and one of the demon's heads fell off. The next day, Rabbi Acha chided them: "If a miracle had not occurred, you would have put my life in danger." (Talmud *Kiddushin* 29b)

7. This statement, a compendium of a variety of rabbinic sources, cites the places in which demons dwell and sport:

Their sporting places are caper bushes and spearworts, where they dwell in groups of sixty; nut trees, where they form in groups of nine; shady spots on moonlight nights, especially the roofs of houses, under gutters, or near ruins; cemeteries and toilets (there is a special demon of the privey known in Hebrew as "*shayd shel bet ha-kissay*"); water, oil and bread crumbs cast on the ground; and there are persons and things coming near them. (Talmud *Pesachim* 3b; *Berachot* 3a, 62b; *Shabbat* 67a; *Gittin* 70a; *Chullin* 105; *Sanhedrin* 65b)

8. The following statement describes the most dangerous nights for demons:

Especially dangerous are the evenings of Wednesday and of the Sabbath, for then Agrat bat Machlat, the dancing roof demon (*Yalkut Chadash, Keshafim*, 56) haunts the air with the train of eighteen myriads of

messengers of destruction, every one of whom has the
power of doing harm (see Talmud *Pesachim* 112b). On
those nights one would not drink water except out of
white vessels and having recited Psalm 29:3–9 (in it
the "voice of God" is mentioned seven times) or other
magical formulas. (Talmud *Pesachim* 3a)

9. Although demons are usually destructive spirits, in
some cases they can be helpful, saving forces:

The saint Abba Jose of Zaintor saved his town from
harm, when informed by a water demon living nearby
that a dangerous fellow demon made his habitation
there, by causing the inhabitants to go down to the edge
of the water at dawn, equipped with iron rods and spits,
and beat the intruder to death. The blood marked the
spot where he was called. (See Midrash Leviticus
Rabbah, 24)

10. In the following reference we learn that some of the
Babylonian rabbinic authorities employed demons as friendly
spirits, even referring to them on a first name basis: Rabbi
Joseph said, "The demon Joseph told me that Ashmadai, the
king of the demons is appointed over all pairs and a king is
not designated a harmful spirit." (Talmud, *Pesachim* 106a)

11. Demons were generally creators of harm, often causing
disease. In the following passage we learn of the demon that
causes blindness as well as the antidote against it:

Our rabbis taught: A person should not drink water
from rivers or pools at night, and if one drinks, his

blood is on his own head because of the danger. What is the danger? The danger of "*shabriri*" (i.e., demon of blindness). But if he is thirsty, what is the remedy? If a person is with him he should say to him, "So-and-so the son of so-and-so, I am thirsty for water." But if not, let him say to himself, "O so-and-so, my mother told me, 'Beware of shabriri': Shabriri, briri, riri, iri, ri [this is an incantation against the blindness demon that resembles an "abracadabra" amulet, in which each succeeding line is reduced by one letter], I am thirsty for water in a white glass." (Talmud *Pesachim* 112a)

12. In this selection we learn of the demon that brings the disease of the croup to children:

When Rabbi Huna was in possession of some medicament, he would take a pitcherful of it, hang it on the doorpost and say: "Whoever wishes to have some, let that person come and take it." Some report that he knew of a medicine against a disease called *shibta* (often understood to mean a female demon who would bring the croup disease to those who did not wash their hands in the morning), and he would place it on a jug of water, hang the latter outside, and say: "Any person who needs it, let that person come and use it to avoid danger." (Talmud *Taanit* 20b)

13. In this Talmudic statement we learn of the fear of demons at night: It is forbidden for one person to greet another at night for fear that person might be a demon. (Talmud *Megillah* 3a)

DEMONS IN JEWISH MYSTICISM

Jewish mystics made use of many of the Talmudic and
midrashic motifs and developed their particular system of
demonology, based on the notion that there is a realm of
darkness and evil in God's world that even God cannot
reach. This dark world is filled with evil spirits, with Lilith
linked to her husband Samael (often identified as the Angel
of Death himself). Castillian kabbalists link the existence of
demons themselves with the last grade of the powers of the
left-side emanation (*sitra achra*) which corresponds to its
ten *sefirot* of evil to the ten holy Sefirot. This contrasts with
the *Zohar*, the book of Jewish mysticism that follows the
Talmudic legend that connects the origin of demons in
sexual intercourse between humans and demonic powers.
This sexual element in the relationship of humans and
demons plays a leading role in the demonology of the
Zohar. In later mystical writings it is explained that demons
born to humans create illegitimate sons, called *banim
shovavim* (i.e., mischievous sons). At death, these sons are
prone to come to accompany the dead person and to claim
their inheritance share. They may also attempt to injure the
legitimate children. This notion has given rise to a cemetery
custom of circling the dead in order to repulse the demons.

SPECIFIC DEMONS

In the Bible foreign gods are called *shedim*, often rendered
as demons in translation. For instance, in Psalm 106:37 we

are told that the people "sacrificed their sons and daughters to the demons." This greatly angered God, causing God to allow the enemies of the Israelites to defeat and oppress them.

Some demons are specifically mentioned by name, and have a somewhat illustrious history in postbiblical literature. The following is a summary of some of the more well-known specific demons in the world of Jewish demonology:

Resheph

Resheph was the Canaanite netherworld god of pestilence. Although not specifically mentioned in the Bible as a god, the name does appear in the Bible. In both Deuteronomy 32:24 and Habakkuk 3:5 "resheph" appears as a synonym for pestilence.

Azazel

The Israelite biblical conception of demons resembled in a number of ways the conception of demons in other cultures. For example, we learn that demons lived in deserts. In the annual ritual ceremony of purification in the ancient sanctuary, Aaron is told to offer two goats, one to God and the other for Azazel, and the goat was to be sent into the wilderness (Leviticus 16:1–10). Many Bible critics, including Nachmonides and Ibn Ezra, share the view that "Azazel" is the name of a demon in the wilderness.

Dever

In Psalm 91:5–6, we are told the following: "You need not fear the terror (*pachad*) of night, the arrow (*chetz*) that flights by day. The pestilence (*dever*) that prowls in the dark, the scourge (*ketev*) that stalks at noon."

Some Bible commentators have associated the Hebrew word *dever* as indicating the demon of pestilence. Others have identified all of the Hebrew words in quotations above as quite likely being associated with the name of demons.

Agrat bat Machlat

This female demon seems to be the mistress of the sorceresses who communicated magic secrets to Amemar (see Talmud *Pesachim* 110a and 112b.)

Lilith:

In the Bible and Talmud

One female demon that is assigned a major central position in Jewish demonology is that of Lilith. Today there is even a popular Jewish feminist magazine named after her. She is often traced to Babylonian demonology, which identifies similar male and female spirits—Lilu and Lilitur.

The first and only Biblical reference to Lilith is in the Book of Isaiah 34:14, where she is listed as one of the spirits that will lay waste to the land on the day of vengeance:

> Wildcats will meet hyenas,
> And the satyr shall cry to his fellow
> Yea, Lilith shall repose there
> And shall find her a place of rest.

Lilith is mentioned several times in the Talmud, in the following contexts. In the Talmud, *Eruvin* 100b, she appears as a female demon with a woman's face, long hair, and wings. We learn in the Talmudic tractate of *Shabbat* 151b that according to Rabbi Haninah, a person sleeping alone in a house is liable to be seized by Lilith. In the Talmud *Bava Batra* 73a we are told that the demon Hormin is one of Lilith's sons.

A female demon who is known by tens of thousands of names and moves about the world at night, visiting women in childbirth with the intent of strangling their newborn children is mentioned in the third-century Greek book *Testament of Solomon*, a book of the Pseudepigrapha. Here she is called Obizoth, and it is related that one of the mystical names of the guardian angel Raphael inscribed on an amulet will prevent her from doing any serious damage or inflicting injury upon another.

In the Midrash

There are numerous rabbinic legends regarding Lilith. For instance, in the *Alphabet of Ben Sira*, a tenth-century work, a legend appears that attempts to explain the widespread custom of writing amulets against Lilith. In this work she is identified with the "first Eve," who was created from the earth at the same time as Adam, and who, unwilling to forgo her equality, disputed with him the manner of their intercourse. Pronouncing God's Name, she flew off into the air. Adam then requested that God send three angels, Snwy, Snsnwy and Smnglf, after her. Locating her at the Red Sea, the angels threatened that if she did not return, one hundred of her sons would die every day. She refused, stating that the very nature of her existence was to harm newborn infants. However, she was forced to swear that whenever she saw the image of those angels in an amulet, she would lose her power over the infant.

In the Midrash of Numbers Rabbah (end of chapter 16), we are told that Lilith turns upon her own children when she finds no children born. This particular motif is said to relate her to the Babylonian Lamashtu.

In Kabbalah

In mystical tradition, Lilith has two basic roles: one who strangles children and one who seduces men, resulting in nocturnal emissions. Through these emissions she bears a never-ending number of demonic children. She is numbered among the four mothers of the demons, the others being Agrat, Machalath, and Naamah. In addition, she becomes the permanent partner of Samael, queen of the realm of the evil forces. In this world of evil she is the mother of the unholy folk, ruling over all that is impure.

Lilith has also been identified with the Queen of Sheba, based on a Jewish and Arab myth that the Queen of Sheba was actually a jinn, half human and half demon. Although no one knows for sure the exact reason for this connection, there is a fair amount of interesting conjecture. It may well be related to the fact that in the first chapter of the Book of Job (1:15) we are told that his seven sons and three daughters were slain by force from Sheba. The *Targum*, the Aramaic translation of the Hebrew Bible, understands Lilith as the instigating force that caused the destruction of Job's children. In Ashkenazic folklore she is depicted as a snatcher of children, a demonic witch, and a seductive dancer.

In the Kabbalah (*Zohar, Ra'aya Meheimna III, 227b*) influenced by astrology, Lilith is related to the planet Saturn and all those of a melancholy disposition—of a "black humor"—are her sons. From the sixteenth century it was believed that if a baby laughed in its sleep that it was an indication that Lilith was playing with him, and it was thus advisable to tap him on the nose to avert danger.

It gradually became quite common to protect women who were giving birth from Lilith's great power by placing amulets over the bed or on all four walls of the room. According to *Shimmush Tehillim*, a book dating from the geonic period, amulets written for women who used to lose their children customarily include Psalm 126 (later replaced by Psalm 121) and the names of the three angels Sanvei, Sansanavei, and Samangalaf.

Asmodeus (Ashmedai)

All of the demons were believed to be under the dominion of a chief called Asmodeus. Said to be derived from the Persian *aesmadiv* (i.e., spirit of anger), Asmodeus is described as king of the demons in the Talmud *Pesachim* 110a: Rabbi Joseph said: "The demon Joseph told me that Ashmedai the king of the demons is appointed over all pairs."

Interestingly, the Talmud in the main does not describe Asmodeus as only an evil doer. In the well-known Talmudic account in the tractate of *Gittin* 69a,b, although Asmodeus usurps the throne of King Solomon, he provides the king with the *shamir*, a magical worm whose touch splits rocks, enabling Solomon's workers to hew stones for the Temple in Jerusalem without the use of prohibited tools of iron.

Asmodeus is also described in the Talmud (*Gittin* 8a) as "rising every day from his dwelling place on the mountain to the firmament," where he "studies in the Academy on

High." As a result of this daily practice, he gains knowledge of the fate of human beings, which oftentimes causes him to act in an enigmatic fashion. For example, while on his way to Solomon, Asmodeus weeps upon seeing a wedding party, later explaining that the bridegroom has only a small amount of time to live. Similarly, on the same journey, he sets a drunkard on the right path in order that he might have a share in the world to come.

Asmodeus first appears in the apocryphal book of Tobit (3:8–17), which describes how in a fit of jealousy he slaughters the successive husbands of a young girl. He is later portrayed as a lawbreaker and the creator of discord between husband and wife in the first-century work *The Testament of Solomon.* Throughout later legendary works, he is for the most part portrayed as mischievous and promiscuous, an almost degraded humorous hero.

Various speculations have been made on the demise of the king of the demons. There is a tradition that he died a martyr's death with the Jews of Mainz in 1096. Another mystical viewpoint is that Asmodeus is merely the title of the office of the king of the demons, just as Pharaoh is the title of the office of the king of Egypt, and that every king of the demons is called Asmodeus. (The word Asmodeus, in *gematriah*, has the same numerical equivalent as that of Pharaoh!)

HOW TO AVOID DEMONS

There have been many activities devised through the ages by which to eradicate and avoid the demons. The observance of the Law was clearly one of the best prophylactics against demons. Wearing *tefillin* (phylacteries), affixing a *mezuzah* to one's doorpost, and the putting on of *tzizit* (prayer shawl fringes) while directly observing the Law were regarded by the rabbis as safeguards against all evil powers (see Talmud *Berachot* 5a). The Midrash Numbers Rabbah 9:5 mentions that a priest's blessing is a protection against evil forces, while the Midrash Exodus Rabbah 32 presents the idea that "when a person performs one *mitzvah*, the Holy Blessed One gives that person one angel to guard him . . .", and that "when a person performs two *mitzvot*, God gives that person two angels to guard him."

In the Mishneh (*Shabbat* 6:2 and *Shekalim* 3:2) amulets are mentioned as being worn for the curative power they were believed to possess. A protective force was attributed to inscribed amulets, often folded with mystical writings in them in addition to magical symbols. The construction of amulets and magical incantations as devices to help ward off evil spirits has a fascinating literature. Many amulets included various combinations and permutations of the letters of different names of God. Names of angels were also used as well. Pictures depicted on various amulets often included the star of David, the *menorah*, as well as an outstretched hand. Three Biblical verses (Exodus 14:19–21) were believed to have strong mystical significance, because each of them consists of seventy-two letters of one of the mysterious names of God. Hence, these verses were assumed to represent the ineffable Divine Name. They were inserted in the amulets in varied forms as an appeal to God for protection.

Other devices for warding off demons included the following: carrying lit torches at night; buying them off with gifts and bribes; deceiving them using disguises; piety and having a good family name; biblical readings, especially Psalm 91; blowing the ram's horn; onions, garlic, leeks, and spices; the colors red and blue; sweet things; keeping a knife on hand; rinsing with running water; keeping one's house clean and tidy; and spitting three times.

THE EVIL EYE

The terms *ayin hara* and *ayn hara* essentially denote envy, jealousy, and greed. In the Hebrew Bible we are told not to dine with a person who is stingy (*ayn ra*) and not to desire that person's delicacies. Opposed to the grudging person is the generous person (*tov ayin*) [Proverbs 22:9]. In the *Ethics of the Fathers* (2:13–14) we are told that a good eye (*ayin tovah*), or generosity, is the best quality to which a person should cling, and that an evil eye (*ayn hara*) is the worst quality, which a person ought to shun.

Over the course of time, it becomes a widespread belief that an envious or begrudging glance of the eye could work evil upon the person to whom it was directed. According to a statement from the Talmud, *Bava Metziah* 107b: Ninety-nine out of a hundred die of an evil eye.

There are numerous midrashic references to the evil eye. In Genesis Rabbah 45:5–6, we learn that Rabbi Hoshaya believed that the evil eye took possession of Hagar causing her to miscarry. Later in Genesis Rabbah 53:13, we are told that Sarah cast an evil eye upon Ishmael, causing him to be seized with feverish pains. Rabbi Jose, the son of Rabbi

Haninah stated (Genesis Rabbah 56:11) that after Abraham had substituted a ram for sacrificial purposes rather than his son Isaac, he sent Isaac home at night, fearing the evil eye.

In the Midrash Leviticus Rabbah 17:3, there is a litany of ten things that are mentioned in connection with causing the dreaded biblical disease of leprosy. The last on the list is the evil eye! Further in the Midrash of Leviticus Rabbah (26:7) we are told that if a man goes to a feast, he does not take his children with him, fearing the evil eye.

In the Midrash of Numbers Rabbah 12:4, we learn that when a king is about to give his daughter in marriage, he gives her an amulet and says to her: "Keep the amulet upon you so that the evil eye may have no power over you any more."

In the Midrash of Deuteronomy Rabbah 1:25, commenting on the phrase "For I have delivered them into your hands," we are told that Og, King of Bashan, began to cast an evil eye upon the Israelites. God interceded and said to him: "Why do you cast your evil eye upon My children? May your eye run out; you are destined to fall by their hand."

Finally, the evil eye is said to have caused the breaking of the first tablets of the Law in the Midrash Numbers Rabbah 12:4 and the death of Daniel's three companions (Chananiah, Mishael, and Azariah) in the Talmud *Sanhedrin* 93a.

The power of the evil eye was not only confined to evildoers. Sometimes, rabbinic heroes were able to use the power of the eye for benevolent purposes. For instance, Rabbi Shimon ben Yochai is described as transforming an evil person into a "heap of bones" by means of his amazing ability (Talmud *Shabbat* 34a) and with the glance of an eye Rabbi Yochanan was able to kill a man who uttered malicious statements about Jerusalem (Talmud *Bava Batra* 75a).

The Code of Jewish Law (chapter 23 of the *Code of Jewish Law*, Ganzfried's Abridged Version) states that two brothers, whether of one father or of one mother, may not be called up to the Torah in succession; nor could a father and son, or grandson be called up in succession, because of the evil eye.

Finally, the Midrash Tanchuma 66 states that "a person will call his handsome son "Ethiop" (in Hebrew, *kushee*) in order to avoid casting the evil eye upon him.

HOW TO AVOID THE EVIL EYE

Many folk beliefs and customs are evident, even today, that work to ameliorate the deleterious effects of the evil eye. Measures taken to avert the evil eye come in two forms. The first is preventative, where the belief exists that the evil eye is activated by arousing the jealousy of the so-called endowed people. This measure calls for preventative measures of self-restraint, such as the avoidance of an expression of praise for a handsome newborn, one who is especially susceptible to the evil eye. The other form is counteractive, meaning that once the evil eye has been activated and the threat of danger is imminent, there is no need for a preventative measure, but rather an immediate confrontation using countermagic, which works to deceive or ultimately defeat the evil eye.

The following is a cross-section of some of the ways of averting the evil eye.

Preventative Measures

1. Do not spread a costly garment over the bed when guests are visiting a house, as "it will be burned by the eye of the guests." (Talmud *Bava Metziah* 30a)

2. Break precious glass at a wedding to avert the evil eye.

3. Veil your beauty, and do not exhibit your riches, all of which are susceptible to the evil eye.

4. Tie a red band around the wrist or neck of a newborn to avert the evil eye.

5. Wear a *chamsa* (from the Arabic word for "five"; an amulet that looks like a hand often containing the evil eye in its center) around your neck for continuous protection from the evil eye.

6. Use an outstretched arm to try to avert the evil eye.

7. Use a mirror or a specific color (red or blue) to continuously reflect the potential glance of the evil eye.

8. Avoid double weddings in one household!

9. Never use the term "evil eye" in conversation. Instead, use the term "good eye" as a euphemism in its place.

10. Never count people using one, two, three, etc. because numbering people creates a special susceptibility to the evil eye. If you need to count people, count "not one," "not two," and so on.

11. If taking your child to school for his or her first time, screen your child with your cloak.

12. Never mention the birth date or the exact age of a person.

13. Wear an amulet inscribed with different names of God and good angels. You may also choose a protective verse, such as Genesis 49:22, believed to be a potent antidote to the evil eye: "Joseph is a fruitful vine, a fruitful vine by a fountain." (Note: The Hebrew word for "vine" (*ayin*) is also the Hebrew word for "eye.")

14. Put a piece of Passover matzah into the pocket of a particularly handsome child to protect him or her against the evil eye.

15. Because fish live beneath the water's surface and cannot be seen, they are, according to the Talmud *Berachot* 20a, immune from the effects of the evil eye. Therefore, putting them on an amulet ought to be quite effective!

16. The "fig" figure, a phallic symbol represented by the thumb thrust out between the first and second fingers will work to avert the evil eye.

Counteractive Measures

1. "Whoever is afraid of the evil eye should stick his right thumb in his left hand and his left thumb in his right hand, proclaiming: 'I, so and so, son of so and so, am of the seed of Joseph, whom the evil eye may not affect.'" (Talmud *Berachot* 55b)

2. To divert the glance from the intended target, hang interesting objects (e.g., precious stones) between the eyes of the endangered person. (*Tosef Shabbat* 4:5)

3. Qualify any praise that you give a beautiful object or person with the phrase *keyn ayen hore* (i.e., may there be no evil eye), often shortened to *kaynahora*.

DREAMS

Almost all people dream, and it has been established that dreams are a necessary outlet for the mind. From the earliest of times, dreams have tantalized people with their secrets, as they were often thought to be signs from divine powers exposing their intent. Ancient Babylonians had implicit trust in dreams as a means of guidance. On the eve of important decisions they slept in temples, hoping for dream counsel. Professional dream interpreters were prominent in ancient Mesopotamia and Egypt, and manuals have revealed hundreds of dream interpretations. The interpretation of dreams has been a major component since the inception of that discipline. Freud and his many successors have spent years of study applying their knowledge to the study of dreams. The Greek philosopher Aristotle believed that because most people find some significance to the dreams that they have dreamt that this is grounds for believing that their supposition is based on experience.

What does Judaism have to say about dreams? What are the theories of dream study that complement that of Jewish thought?

On the whole, the Bible says remarkably little on the subject of dream interpretation. Only Joseph and Daniel engage in it, and both give the credit unreservedly to God. In the Talmud, Midrash, *Aggadah*, works of philosophy, and Jewish law codes, there is a wealth of varying opinion concerning dreams. This chapter introduces you to the world of dreams and the language that they speak.

IN THE BIBLE

The biblical view of dreams agrees for the most part with the view of many ancient people, namely that dreams are visions of things actually transpiring and that they are often regarded as signs or omens. Often replete with many symbolic images, dreams are often considered to be divine communication of facts that will in the future be historically actualized. Throughout the Bible, they are best understood by prophets and visionaries who are able to connect themselves to the divine "wire of communication," so to speak.

In one of the earliest references to dreams in the Bible, Avimelech, the king of Gerar takes Sarah, Abraham's wife, into his harem. In a dream revelation he is charged with the forcible abduction of a married woman. Avimelech defends his innocence on two grounds: He has not had sexual relations with her and the information about her married status was withheld from him by the parties concerned. God counters the first argument by asserting that it was He who prevented the violation of Sarah. As to the second, the king's integrity is put to the test. Here is the text of this dream sequence:

But God came to Avimelech in a dream of the night, and said to him: "Behold, you shall die, because of the woman that you have taken, for she is a man's wife." Now Avimelech had not come near her, and he said: "Lord, will you slay even a righteous nation? Did he not say to me: She is my sister? and she, even she herself said: He is my brother. In the simplicity of my heart and the innocence of my hands have I done this." And God said to him in the dream: "Yea, I know in the simplicity of your heart that you have done this, and I also withheld you from sinning against me. Therefore I did not make you suffer. Now therefore, restore the man's wife . . ." (Genesis 20:3–7)

At the conclusion of Avimelech's dream, Avimelech is described as presenting Abraham with sheep, oxen, and servants and returns his wife to him.

Dreams that occur in sacred places are considered to be revelations from the resident deity. People in search of divine direction resort to such shrines and sleep on the premises. This was a widespread practice for people of the ancient Near East. One of the clearest instances of this type of dream is that which occurs to Jacob upon his taking leave from Beer Sheba. Lighting up at a certain place, Jacob stops for the night and goes to sleep. (It was customary throughout the world of the ancient Near East for a devotee to sleep in the sacred precincts of a temple in order to induce the deity to reveal its will.) In our story, it is God who will take the initiative in revealing Himself to the amazed Jacob:

He came upon a certain place and stopped there for the night, for the sun had set. Taking one of the stones of that place, he put it under his head and lay down in that place. He had a dream: a stairway was set on the ground and its top reached to the sky, and angels of God were going up and down on it. And God was standing beside him and God said, "I am the Lord, the God of your father Abraham and the God of Isaac. The ground on which you are lying I will assign to you and to your offspring. Your descendants shall be as the dust of the earth. You shall spread out to the west and to the east, to the north and south. All the families of the earth shall bless themselves by you and your descendants. Remember, I am with you, and I will protect you wherever you go and I will bring you back to this land. I will not leave you until I have done what I have promised you." Jacob awoke from his sleep and said, "Surely the Lord is in this place, and I did not know it." Shaken, he said, "How awesome is this place. This is none other than the abode of God, and that is the gateway to heaven." (Genesis 28:11–16)

Visual imagery and an auditory sensation are the manifest content of Jacob's dream. Although the angels play no role in the dream, some commentators have suggested that their presence may symbolize Jacob's personal hopes and fears and his prayer for protection that rise to heaven and do receive a response.

One of the first biblical examples of several dreams that are filled with symbolism is that of Joseph, often known in Jewish tradition as "the dreamer." In the Joseph narrative, which occurs in the Book of Genesis, six dreams occur— two by Joseph, two by the prisoners, and two by Pharaoh all of which lend suspense to the story. In the dreams previously described, the revelatory message is conveyed verbally. In the case of Joseph's dreams, God does not figure explicitly in the dreams' content, although it is clearly taken for granted that God is the source of the message being conveyed in the dream. Because the predictive aspect of dreams was considered valid in the ancient world, Joseph's brothers take his dreams seriously after hearing them.

Here are the texts of the first two dreams of Joseph:

> Joseph said to them, "Hear the dream which I have dreamed: There we were binding sheaves in the field, when suddenly my sheaf stood up and remained upright. Then your sheaves gathered around and bowed down to my sheaf." His brothers answered, "Do you mean to reign over us? Do you mean to rule over us?" And they hated him even more for his talk about his dreams. (Genesis 37:6–8)

> He dreamed another dream and told it to his brothers, saying, "Look, I have had another dream. This time, the sun, moon and the eleven stars were bowing down to me." And when he told it to his father and brothers, his father berated him. "What," he said to him, "is this dream you have dreamed? Are we to come, I and your mother and your brothers, and bow low to you to the ground?" So his brothers were angry with him, and his father kept the matter in mind. (Genesis 37:9–11)

These two dreams are self-explanatory to Joseph's brothers, in contrast to those that will follow that require an interpreter in order to extract their meaning. In these dreams there is a clear assertion of authority by Joseph and of acquiescence on the part of his brothers.

The next pair of dreams occur when Joseph is in the land of Egypt after having been sold into slavery. Two of the chief officials of King Pharaoh, the cupbearer and the royal baker who have been confined to prison, have dreams. Here they are in the words of the biblical narrative:

> They said to Joseph, "We had dreams, and there is no one to interpret them." So Joseph said to them, "Surely God can interpret. Tell me your dreams." Then the chief cupbearer told his dream to Joseph. He said to him, "In my dream, there was a vine in front of me. On the vine were three branches. It had barely budded, when out came its blossoms and its clusters ripened into grapes. Pharaoh's cup was in my hand, and I took the grapes, pressed them into Pharaoh's cup, and placed the cup in Pharaoh's hand." Joseph said to him, "This is its interpretation: The three branches are three days. In three days Pharaoh will pardon you and restore you to your post. You will place Pharaoh's cup in his hand, as was your custom formerly when you were his cupbearer." (Genesis 40:8–13)

What makes this dream interpretion noteworthy is the fact that Joseph credits God with his ability to decipher the dreams.

When the chief baker saw how favorably it had been interpreted, he described to him his dream:

> "In my dream, similarly, there were three openwork baskets on my head. In the uppermost basket were all kinds of food for Pharaoh that a baker prepares. The birds were eating out of the basket above my head." Joseph answered, "This is its interpretation: The three baskets are three days. In three days Pharaoh will lift

off your head and impale you upon a pole. The birds
will pick off your flesh." (Genesis 40:16–19)

Indeed, both interpretations of Joseph came true. The
chief cupbearer was restored to his position, as the chief
baker was impaled, just as Joseph had interpreted.

The next pair of dreams belong to none other than
Pharaoh himself. Here are the texts of his dreams:

After two years' time, Pharaoh dreamed that he was
standing by the Nile, when out of the Nile there came
up seven cows, handsome and sturdy, and they grazed
in reed grass. But presently, seven other cows came up
from the Nile close behind them, ugly and gaunt, and
stood beside the cows on the banks of the Nile. The
ugly gaunt cows ate up the seven handsome sturdy
ones. And Pharaoh awoke. He fell asleep and dreamed
a second time. Seven ears of grain, solid and healthy,
grew on a single stalk. But close behind them sprouted
seven ears, thin and scorched by the east wind. And the
thin ears swallowed up the seven solid and full ears.
Then Pharaoh awoke . . . Joseph said to Pharaoh,
"Pharaoh's dreams are one and the same: God has told
Pharaoh what He is about to do. The seven healthy
cows are seven years, and the seven healthy ears are
seven years. It is the same dream. The seven lean and
ugly cows that followed are seven years, as are also the
seven empty ears scorched by the east wine. They are
seven years of famine. It is just as I have told Pharaoh:
God has revealed to Pharaoh what He is about to do.
Immediately ahead are seven years of great abundance
in the land of Egypt. After them will come seven years
of famine, and all the abundance in the land of Egypt

will be forgotten. As the land is ravaged by famine no trace of the abundance will be left in the land because of the famine thereafter, for it will be very severe. As for Pharaoh having the same dream twice, it means that the matter has been determined by God, and that God will carry it out." (Genesis 41:1–7 and 25–32)

Following Joseph's interpretation, he suggests to Pharaoh several measures that need to be taken to avert the menace of the famine: the selection of a national commissioner, the appointment of regional overseers, and the institution of urban grain storage. The advice is presented not as part of the dream message, but as a personal suggestion. The plan pleases Pharaoh, and he says to his courtiers the following astounding statement: "Could we find another like him, a man in whom is the spirit of God?" This is the first biblical mention of a person so endowed with the spirit of God, and soon Pharaoh promotes Joseph based on his ability interpret dreams to the position of Grand Vizier of Egypt.

What is clear from these dream texts and Joseph's interpretation is that Joseph all along was divinely directed and he left no detail of any dream undeciphered.

DREAMS IN THE BOOK OF DANIEL

There are numerous dreams in the Book of Daniel, known for its symbolic representations and predictions. Chapter 2 of the book tells how, in the second year of King Nebuchadnezzar's reign, Daniel interpreted his dream of a colossal image and was elevated to high rank in the royal service. Here is a portion of this text:

In the second year of the reign of Nebuchadnezzar, Nebuchadnezzar dreamed dreams. His spirit was troubled and his sleep broke from him. The king commanded to call the magicians, the enchanters, and the sorcerers, and the Chaldeans, to tell the king his dreams. So they came and stood before the king. The king said to them: "I have dreamed a dream, and my spirit is troubled to know the dream. . . ." As for you, O king, your thoughts come into your mind upon your bed, what should come to pass hereafter; and He that reveals secrets has made known to you what shall come to pass . . . You, O king, saw and beheld a great image. This image, which was mighty, and whose brightness was surpassing, stood before you; and the appearance was terrible. As for that image, its head was of fine gold, its breast and its arm of silver, its belly and its thighs of brass. Its legs of iron, its feet part of iron, and part of clay. You saw too that a stone was cut out without hands, which smote the image upon its feet that were ore iron and clay, and broke them in pieces. Then was the iron, the clay, the brass, the silver and the gold, broken in pieces together, and became like the chaff of the summer threshing floors; and the wind carried them away, so that no place was found for them; and the stone that smote the image became a great mountain, and filled the whole earth. This is the dream and we will tell the interpretation to the king. You, O king of kings, unto whom the God of heaven has given the kingdom, the power, the strength and glory. And wheresoever the children of men, the beasts of the field, and the fowls of the heaven dwell, has God given them into Your hand, and has made you to rule over them. You are the head of gold. And after you shall arise another kingdom inferior to you. And another third kingdom of brass, which shall bear rule over all the earth. And the fourth kingdom shall be as strong as iron. . . .Then King Nebuchadnezzar fell upon his face and worshiped Daniel, and commanded that they should offer an offering and sweet odors for him. The King spoke to Daniel and said: "Of a truth it is, that your God is the God of gods, and the Lord of kings, and a revealer of secrets, seeing you have been able to reveal this secret." (Daniel 2:1–3, 29, 31–40, 46–48)

After the interpretation of King Nebuchadnezzar's dream comes the climax of the entire episode. The God of Israel is acclaimed by the greatest ruler on earth as the supreme God of the universe. Nebuchadnezzar assures Daniel that he is conscious of the reality of God's supremacy, and Daniel, like Joseph in Egypt, is promoted to rule over the whole province of Babylon.

Chapter 4 of the Book of Daniel recounts yet another instance of Daniel's ability to interpret dreams. This time King Nebuchadnezzar dreams of a gigantic tree, the significance of which Daniel reveals to him:

The tree that you saw, which grew and was strong, whose height reached heaven, and the sight thereof to all the earth; whose leaves were fair, and the fruit thereof much, and in it was food for all; under which the beasts of the field dwelt, and upon whose branches the fowls of the heaven had their habitation. It is you, O king, that are grown and become strong. For your greatness is grown, and reaches to heaven, and your dominion to the end of the earth. And whereas the king saw a watcher and a holy one coming down from heaven, and saying: Hew down the tree and destroy it; nevertheless, leave the stump of the roots thereof in the earth, even in a band of iron and brass, in the tender grass of the field; and let it be wet with the dew of heaven, and let his portion be with the beasts of the field, til seven times pass over him. This is the interpretation, O king, and it is the decree of the Most High, which is come upon my lord the king. That you shall be driven from men, and your dwelling shall be with the beasts of the field, and you shall be made to eat grass as oxen and you shall be wet with the dew of heaven and seven times shall pass over you; till you know that the Most High rules in the kingdom of men, and gives it to whomsoever He wishes. And whereas it was commanded to leave the stump of the roots of the tree, your kingdom shall be sure unto you, after that you shall have known that the heavens do rule. (Daniel 4:17–23)

After Nebuchadnezzar was driven from men and his body was wet with the dew of heaven as Daniel had predicted in his interpretation of the dream, Nebuchadnezzar blesses God and again recognizes God's Sovereignty, which he had before flouted.

Each of Nebuchadnezzar's dreams is marked by symbolism corresponding to future events, all of which subsequently came to pass.

OTHER STATEMENTS RELATED TO DREAMS IN THE BIBLE

Throughout the Bible there are shorter instances where the nature of the dream and its import is discussed. For instance, the Bible tells how Laban was administered a heavenly warning not to harm Jacob in a dream. The Bible itself actually makes an analogy between dreams and prophecy, saying, "If there appears among you a prophet or dreamer of dreams and he gives you a sign or portent saying, Let us follow and worship another god whom you have not experienced, do not heed the words of that prophet or dreamer of dreams" (Deuteronomy 13:2–3).

We are also told in the Bible how Gideon took a dream as a sign from God that he would be victorious in battle, after overhearing an enemy soldier discuss his dream of imminent defeat at Gideon's hands. King Saul "inquired of the Lord, and the Lord did not answer, neither by dreams nor by the *urim* nor through a prophet" (I Samuel 28:6).

In the Book of Job, Elihu underscores the use of dreams as a medium for supernatural communication with his statement: "Surely God speaks once, even twice, yet man perceives it not. In a dream, in a vision of the night . . ." (Job 33:14–15).

The dependability of a prophetic message is also mentioned by the Prophet Joel, who states, "And it shall come to pass afterward that I will pour out My spirit upon all flesh, and your sons and daughter shall prophesy, your old men shall dream dreams, your young men shall see visions" (Joel 3:1).

Finally, in the Book of Jeremiah 23:25 and in the Book of Zechariah 10:2, false dreams are described. Dreams that are deemed false are those that are not subsequently realized or those that never occurred at all. The Book of Ecclesiastes likened the content of a dream to the conversation of a fool: "For a dream comes through a multitude of business; and a fool's voice is known by a multitude of works" (Ecclesiastes 5:2). Likewise it is written, "Too many dreams and nonsense" (Ecclesiastes 5:3). In the same vein Isaiah asserts, "It shall be even as when a hungry man dreams, and behold, he eats; but he awakes and his soul is empty. Or as when a thirsty man dreams, and behold, he drinks, but awakes and his soul longs for water—so shall the multitude of all the nations be that fight against Mount Zion" (Isaiah 29:8). Thus, according to Isaiah in this passage, although a dream can at times appear very promising, it nonetheless leaves the dreamer empty, because in essence it is merely an illusion.

DREAMS IN THE TALMUD
AND RABBINIC COMMENTARY

Many famous Talmudic teachers frequently discussed dreams and enunciated doctrines concerning them. Yochanan ben Zakkai, for example, dreamed that his sister's sons would lose seven hundred *deanrii* in that year. He therefore pressed them to give alms frequently, so that they might lose that sum piecemeal in a noble way (Talmud Bava Batra, 10a).

Diametrically opposed views on dreams were often expressed by the rabbinic sages. Jonathan stated that "a man is shown in a dream only what is suggested by his own thoughts" (Talmud *Berachot* 55b). This statement corresponds to the view of Freud, who asserts that certain thoughts that are suppressed during the day may reappear in a dream, where they find fulfillment. As the Talmud (*Berachot* 55b) asserts, "A dream is only the result of the thought pondered during the day . . . Rava says that this is proven by the fact that a person never sees in a dream a tree of gold or an elephant passing through the eye of a needle"

(Talmud *Berachot* 55b). In other words, farfetched thoughts are not likely to be envisioned in a dream.

That dreams are the result of one's thoughts during the course of the day may also be noted from what the Talmud relates concerning Rabbi Joshua and Rabbi Samuel:

> The Emperor of Rome said to Rabbi Joshua, the son of Rabbi Chaninia, "You Jews profess to be very clever. Tell me what I shall see in my dream tonight." Rabbi Joshua said to him, "You will see the Persians making you do forced labor, and despoiling you and making you feed unclean animals with a golden crook." He thought about it all day, and in the night he saw it in his dream. King Shapur I said to Samuel, "You profess to be very clever. Tell me what I shall see in my dream tonight." He said to him, "You will see the Romans coming and taking you captive and making you grind date stones in a golden mill." He thought about it all day, and in the night he saw it in a dream. (Talmud *Berachot* 56a)

It is also told of Rabbis Meir and Nathan that after behaving naughtily toward Simeon ben Gamliel, "they were told in their dreams to go and pacify them. Nathan went, but Rabbi Meir did not, saying "Dreams are of no consequence" (Talmud *Horayot* 13b).

The extent to which the sages did not place a lot of value on dreams is demonstrated by Chanan's statement that "even if the genius of dreams informs a man that on the morrow he will die, he should not desist from prayer, since it is said [Ecclesiastes 5:6]: 'For through the multitude of dreams and vanities there are also many words; but fear God'" (Talmud *Berachot* 10b).

There were, however, sages that did believe in the efficacy of dreams, regarding them in the nature of prophecy. For example, Rabbi Haninah ben Isaac declared that "a dream is a variety of prophecy" (Genesis Rabbah 17:5). Rabbi Joseph said that "if one was placed under a ban in a dream, ten persons are necessary for lifting the ban" (Talmud *Nedarim* 8a).

Fasting became customary in rabbinic times when a person had a so-called bad dream. Called in Hebrew the *ta'anit chalom*, Rav once asserted: "Fasting is as potent against a dream as fire is against a tow" (Talmud *Shabbat* 11a).

The Talmud (*Berachot* 55b) records that there were twenty-four professional interpreters of dreams in Jerusalem, clearly an indication that the masses did indeed believe in the power and symbolism of dreams.

Another view regarded dreams as composed alike of truth and of incidental features. This view was expressed by Rabbi Yochanan in the name of Simeon ben Yochai: "Just as there can be no grain without straw, so there can be no dream without meaningless matter" (Talmud *Berachot* 55a). Berachiah is quoted with a similar viewpoint: "While part of a dream may be fulfilled, the whole of it never is fulfilled" (Talmud *Berachot* 55a).

Sometimes sages distinguished between dreams that lacked substance and those that are fulfilled. This was the opinion of Rabbi Yochanan who declared that "three dreams are fulfilled: an early morning dream, a dream which a friend has about one and a dream which is interpreted within a dream" (Talmud *Berachot* 55b).

Another type of dream discussed in rabbinic literature was those whose sources were considered to be the *galgalim*, the celestial spheres. The belief was that when a person sleeps one's body interacts with various celestial bodies. These dreams, caused by the soul's interaction with astrological signs and celestial spheres often revealed future events. According to the biblical commentator Abarbanel commenting on the dreams in the portion of *Mikketz*' (i.e., Genesis 41–44:17), the celestial spheres possess true content and information as to what is decreed upon a person by Heaven. In agreement with Abarbanel was the Ralbag, a noted biblical scholar, who wrote that the supernal spheres are partners in the fate of human beings and God's Will, which regulates every facet of a person's life, is channeled through the celestial spheres. It is entirely possible that this dream type is alluded to by the rabbinic sages who wrote that "a dream is one-sixtieth of prophecy," and that "the unripe fruit of prophecy is a dream" (Genesis Rabbah 17:5).

The Talmudic sages were also known to provide various instructions regarding how to act after having certain dreams. There is a list of verses that are to be recited and actions that are to be taken. Here is one such example from the Talmudic tractate of *Berachot* 56b:

> Rabbi Joshua ben Levi said: If one sees a river in his dreams he should rise early and say, "Behold, I will extend peace to her like a river," before another verse occurs to him: "For distress will come in like a river." [Isaiah 66:12]
>
> If one dreams of a bird, he should rise early and say, "As birds hover, so will the Lord of Hosts protect" before another verse occurs to him: "As a bird wanders from her nest, so is a man that wanders from his place." [Proverbs 27:8]
>
> If one sees a dog in his dream, he should rise early and say, "But against any of the children of Israel shall not

a dog whet his tongue," before another verse occurs to him: "Yea, the dogs are greedy." [Isaiah 56:11]
If one sees a lion in his dreams, he should rise early and say, "The lion has roared, who will not fear?" [Amos 3:8] Before another verse occurs to him: "A lion is gone up from his thicket." [Jeremiah 4:7]

There are a whole host of stories related in rabbinic literature where dreams are the medium not only of a prophetic vision, but for actual communication between the living and the dead.

Here are several examples:

The inhabitants of a city desired to migrate to a new site. The spirit of one of those buried in the cemetery serving the city appeared to one of the city folk in a dream. He bade him to tell his fellow citizens that they should not move away, as the dead derive great pleasure from the visits the city dwellers paid to their graves. If the inhabitants would indeed decide to leave, the apparition continued, they were being warned that their end would be death and destruction. In the end, the warning was not heeded, and they were wiped out. (Sefer *Chassidim* 709)

A great sage had a dream in which he saw a being that was taller than the sage's own house. The being had the face of a man. The tall man said to the sage, "Come and I will show you where the grave of your father lies." The tall man led the sage to the father's gravesite, lifted up the grave corner, and said to the sage, "Now, speak to your father." The sage saw that his father was angry and did not want to speak to him. The tall man

then said to the sage, "Your father does not want to
answer you because his grave was surrounded by
stones, but gentiles came along and took two of them,
and you have not replaced them." The sage looked at
the grave, and two stones were indeed missing. Upon
awakening, the sage proceeded to the cemetery, to find
that his father's grave was missing two stones. He then
saw gentiles who were extracting large stones from the
ground in order to make a foundation for a house. He
approached them and told them he would give them a
modest sum if they would place two of the stones in the
empty space near his father's grave. They did so, and
the dream was not repeated. (Sefer *Chassidim*, 726)

That the sages also viewed dreams as a medium of
communication often used by disembodied forces is appar-
ent in this story by the counsel given by Rabbi Judah the
Chassid to two friends.

The friends were so close that they could not bear to
think of departing from each other even after death.
They swore to one another that whoever died first
would return to his surviving friend and tell him about
life in the world-to-come. How would this come about?
The dead friend would enter the dreams of his living
friend. (Sefer *Chassidim*, 728)

The supreme category of dreams in the Talmud were
those that were divinely inspired. Just as God understands
the ways of every person in every detail, so too many sages
believed that God guides every person to find his or her
individual destiny. This God effects for His messengers—
the prophets, through prophecy, the highest form of divine

communication, as well as for ordinary humans via the form
of dream communication. This form of dream is often
utilized to relate future events, and the greatest incidence of
this dream form was among youths and fools rather than
scholars. (Apparently scholarship so totally preoccupied the
thoughts of scholars that they did not have enough time, so
to speak, to dream.)

Acting on the premise that meaningful dreams are the
focus of God's messages, the rabbinic sages instituted
different verses to be recited upon awakening from a bad
dream. They also instituted a special prayer for the nullification of a dream, known as *hatavat chalom*. In some
synagogues, it is said by the congregants while the priests
bless them, because, according to some views, this portion
of prayer is a time of general good will. Here is the text for
the prayer for the nullification of a dream:

If one has seen a dream and does not remember what
he saw, let him stand before the priests at the time
when they spread out their hands and say as follows:
"Sovereign of the Universe, I am Yours and my dreams
are Yours. I have dreamt a dream and I do not know
what it is. Whether I have dreamt about myself or my
companions have dreamt about me, or I have dreamt
about others, if they are good dreams, confirm them
and reinforce them like the dreams of Joseph. If they
require a remedy, heal them, as the waters of Marah
were healed by Moses, our teacher, and as Miriam was
healed of her leprosy, and Hezekiah of his sickness,
and the waters of Jericho by Elisha. As you did turn the
curse of the wicked Bilaam into a blessing, so turn all
my dreams into something good for me." He should
conclude his prayer along with the priests, so that the

congregation may answer Amen. If he cannot manage
to finish together with the priests, he should say: You
who are majestic on high, who abides in might, You
who are peace and Your name is peace, may it be Your
will to bestow peace upon us. (Talmud *Berachot* 55b)

Another method for dealing with a bad dream is through
the *taanit chalom*, the dream fast. The Talmud (*Taanit* 12b)
states that one should fast after experiencing a worrisome
dream—even on the Sabbath, when it is forbidden to fast.

Furthermore, the Talmud prescribes a procedure for
turning an evil dream into a good one. This procedure is
based on the number three—three verses being recited,
three instances of the dream being good, and so on. This
procedure is related in the Talmud as follows:

Rabbi Huna ben Ammi said in the name of Rabbi
Pedat, who heard it from Rabbi Yochanan: If a person
has a dream which makes him sad, he should go and
have it interpreted in the presence of three. He should
have it interpreted? Has not Rabbi Chisda said: A
dream which is not interpreted is like a letter which is
not read and therefore can do no harm? Say, rather,
then, he should have a good construction given to it in
the presence of three. Let him bring three and say to
them: I have seen a good dream. And they will say to
him: Good it is and good may it be. May the All
Merciful turn it to good. Seven times may it be decreed
from heaven that it should be good and may it be good.
They should say three verses with the word *hafach*
(turn) and three with the word *padach* (redeem) and
three with the word *shalom* (peace). Three with the
word "turn," namely 1. "You did **turn** for me my

mourning into dancing. You did loosen my sackcloth and gird me with gladness." [Psalm 30:12] 2. "Then shall the virgin rejoice in the dance, and the young men and the old together. For I will **turn** their mourning into joy and will comfort them and make them rejoice from their sorrow." [Jeremiah 31:13] 3. "Nevertheless, the Lord your God would not hearken unto Bilaam, but the Lord your God **turned** the curse into a blessing for you." [Deuteronomy 23:6]

Three verses with the word "redeem," namely, 1. "He has **redeemed** my soul in peace, so that none can come near to me." [Psalm 55:19] 2. And the **redeemed** of the Lord shall return and come with singing to Zion . . . and sorrow and sighing shall flee away." [Isaiah 35:10] 3. The people said to Saul, Shall Jonathan die, who has wrought this great salvation in Israel? . . . So the people **redeemed** Jonathan that he died not. [I Samuel 14:45]

Three verses with the word "peace," namely, 1. "**Peace**, peace to him that is far and to him that is near, says the Lord that creates the fruits of the lips; and I will heal him." 2. "Then the spirit clothed Amasai who was chief of the captains: Yours are we, David, and on your side, you, son of Yishai: **Peace**, peace be unto you and peace be your helpers, for your God helps you." [I Chronicles, 12:19) 3. Thus you shall say: all hail, and **peace** be both to you and peace be to your house, and peace be all that you have. (I Samuel 25:6)

In the following story from the Talmud, we see that an interpreter seemingly has the ability to manipulate the message of a dream according to his whims.

Bar Hadaya was an interpreter of dreams. He would give a favorable interpretation to one who paid him a fee and an unfavorable one to one who did not. Abbaye and Rava each had the same dream. Abbaye gave him a *zuz*, and Rava gave him nothing. The two said to him: In our dream, we had read to us the verse, "Your ox shall be slain before your eyes, and you shall not eat of it" [Deuteronomy 28:31]. To Rava, Bar Hadaya said: Your merchandise will depreciate, and because of the distress in your heart, you will be unable to eat. To Abbaye, he said, Your merchandise will appreciate so much that you will be unable to eat because of the joy in your heart. The two reported: We had read to us the verse "You shall carry much seed out into the field, and shall gather little in" (Deuteronomy 28:38). To Abbaye, Bar Hadaya interpreted only the first half of the verse; to Rava, only the second half.

The two reported: We have read to us the verse "And all the peoples of the earth shall see that the Name of the Lord is called upon you; and they shall be afraid of you" (Deuteronomy 28:10).

To Abbaye, Bar Hadaya said: Your fame will go forth, you will become head of the academy, and all people will fear you. To Rava, he said: You will be arrested in the company of robbers, and because of what will be done to you, all will be the more afraid for themselves. The next day, the royal treasury was broken into by robbers, and the authorities arrested Rava. So people were afraid and said: If Rava was arrested, how much more and more are we likely to be.

The two told Bar Hadaya: We saw a head of lettuce lying over the mouth of a cask. To Abbaye, Bar Hadaya said: Your business will double as speedily as the

growth of a lettuce. To Rava, he said: Your business
will prove as bitter as a lettuce. Later, Rava went to Bar
Hadaya by himself and reported: I saw two doves
flying away. Bar Hadaya: You will divorce two wives.
Rava said to him, I saw two turnip tops. He replied:
You will receive two blows with a cudgel. Rava went
and sat out all day in the house of study, where he came
upon two blind men quarreling with each and went to
separate them, and they gave him two blows with their
cudgels. They raised their cudgels to give Rava a third
blow, but he said, "Enough. In my dream I saw only
two."

Finally, Rava went over, paid Bar Hadaya a fee, and
reported: I saw a wall fall down. To which Bar Hadaya
replied: You will acquire wealth without limit.

Rava reported: I saw my own house collapse, and
everyone came and took it away brick by brick. Bar
Hadaya replied, Your teachings will spread throughout
the world.

Rava reported: I dreamed that my head was split open
and my brains spilled out. Bar Hadaya replied: The
feathers stuffed in your pillow will burst out bit by bit.
He reported: In my dream I had the Egyptian Hallel
read to me. Bar Hadaya replied: Miracles will happen
to you.

Once, when Bar Hadaya was traveling with Rava by
ship, he said to himself: Why would I accompany a
man to whom a miracle will happen? As Bar Hadaya
was disembarking, he accidentally dropped a book,
which Rava found. He saw written in it: All dreams
follow the interpreter's mouth. At that, Rava ex-
claimed, "Wretch, it all depended on you, and you

caused me such great distress." (Talmud *Berachot* 56a–b)

In this story, it appears that Bar Hadaya is able to recognize that the dreams under analysis possessed both positive and negative connotations. When one would pay for his interpretation, he would inform that person of the positive but not the negative implications. If the dreamer would not pay, he would inform him of the negative and be silent about the positive implications. The individual with the positive interpretation would look for its fulfillment, and would be oblivious to the negative connotations also contained in the dream, since they were never interpreted, and vice verse. This was a wonderful ploy that helped Bar Hadaya increase his earnings!

Never did Bar Hadaya actually determine the reality. Rather, he influenced the dreamer to look only for the fulfillment of those aspects of the dream that he had interpreted, causing him to forget the remainder of the dream.

DREAM SYMBOLS

The following is a list of various symbols found in a dream and the things that they represent. Perhaps you will find them useful in understanding your own dreams! They are all found in the Talmudic tractate of *Berachot* 56b–57b:

1. If one sees a reed in a dream, he may hope for wisdom. If one sees several reeds, he may hope for understanding. A pumpkin, a palm heart, and a reed are all auspicious in a dream. It has been taught: pumpkins are shown in a dream only to one who fears Heaven with all his might.

2. There are five sayings in connection with an ox in a dream. If one dreams that he eats of his flesh, he will become rich; if that an ox has gored him, he will have sons that will contend together in the study of Torah; if that an ox bit him, sufferings will come upon him; if that he kicked him, he will have to go on a long journey; if that he rode upon one, he will rise to greatness.

3. If one sees a donkey in a dream, he may hope for salvation.

4. If one sees grapes in a dream, if they are white, whether in season or not in season, they are a good sign; if black, in season, they are a good sign. If they are not in season, they are a bad sign.

5. If one sees a white horse in a dream, whether walking gently or galloping, it is a good sign. If a red horse, if walking gently it is a good sign. If galloping, it is a bad sign.

6. If one sees Ishmael in his dream, his prayer will be heard. And it must be Ishmael the son of Abraham, but not an ordinary Arab. If one sees a camel in his dream, death has decreed upon him by Heaven and he has been delivered from it.

7. If one sees Pinchas in a dream, a miracle will be wrought for him. If one sees an elephant in a dream, a miracle will be wrought for him. If several elephants, wonders of wonders will be wrought for him. The elephants are a good sign if saddled, but a bad omen if not saddled.

8. If one sees the words of a funeral oration, mercy will be granted to him from Heaven and he will be redeemed. This is only if he sees the words in writing. If one in a dream answers, "May His great name be blessed," he may be assured that he has a place in the World to Come. If one dreams that he is reciting the *Shema*, he is worthy that the Divine Presence should rest upon him, but his generation is not deserving enough. If one dreams that he is putting on phylacteries, he may look forward to greatness. If one dreams that he is praying, it is a good sign, provided that he does not complete the prayer.

9. If one sees wheat in a dream, he will see peace. If one sees barley in a dream, his iniquities will depart.

10. If one sees in a dream a vine laden with fruit, his wife will not have a miscarriage. If one sees a choice vine, he may look forward to seeing the Messiah.

11. If one sees a fig tree in a dream, his learning will be preserved within him.

12. If one sees pomegranates in a dream, if they are little ones, his business will be fruitful like a pomegranate. If big ones, his business will increase like a pomegranate. If they are split open, if he is a scholar, he may hope to study more Torah. If he is not learned, he may hope to perform more *mitzvot*.

13. If one sees olives in a dream, if they are little ones, his business will continue to prosper, increasing like an olive. This is if he sees the fruit. If he sees the tree, he will have many sons. Some say that if he sees an olive in his dream he will acquire a good name. If one sees palm trees in a dream, his transgressions will come to an end.

14. If one sees a goat in his dream, he will have a blessed year. If several goats, several blessed years.

15. If one sees myrtle in his dream, he will have good luck with his property. If he has no property he will inherit some from elsewhere.

16. If one sees an *etrog* in his dream, he is honored in the sight of his Maker. If one sees a palm branch in his dream, he is single hearted in devotion to his Father in heaven.

17. If one sees a goose in a dream, then he may hope for wisdom. He who dreams of being with one will be head of an academy.

18. If one sees a rooster in a dream, he may expect a male child. If several roosters in a dream, he may expect several sons. If one sees a hen, a fine garden and rejoicing. If one sees eggs in a dream, his petition remains in suspense. If they are broken, his petition will be granted. The same with nuts and cucumbers and all vessels of glass and all breakable things like these.

19. If one dreams that he enters a large town, his desire will be fulfilled.

20. If one dreams that he is shaving his head, it is a good sign for him. If his head and his beard, for him and for all of his family is it a good sign.

21. If one dreams that he is sitting in a small boat, he will acquire a good name. If in a large boat, both he and his family will acquire one, but this is only if it is on the high seas.

22. If one dreams that he is easing himself, it is a good omen for him. But this is only if he did not wipe himself in his dream.

23. If one dreams that he goes up to a roof, he will attain a high position. If that he goes down, he will be degraded. Abaye and Rava, however, both say that once he has attained a high position that he will remain there.

24. If one dreams that he is tearing his garments, his evil decree will be rent. If one dreams that he is standing naked, if in Babylon, he will remain sinless. If in the land of Israel, he will be naked of pious deeds. If one dreams that he has been arrested by the police, protection will be offered him. If that he has been placed in neck chains, additional protection will be afforded him. This is only if he dreams of neck chains, not of mere rope. If one dreams that he walks into a marsh, he will become head of an academy. If into a forest, he will become the head of the collegiates.

25. If one sees a serpent in dream, it means that his living is assured. If it bites him, it means that it will be doubled. If he kills it, he will lose his sustenance.

26. All kinds of drink are a good sign except wine. One may drink it and it turns out well, and one may drink it and it turns out ill. For a scholar, it is always good.

27. There are three kings who are significant in a dream. If one sees David in a dream, he may hope for piety. If Solomon, he may hope for wisdom. If Achav, let him fear for punishment.

28. There are three prophets of significance for dreams. If one sees the Book of Kings, he may look for greatness. If Ezekiel, he may look forward to wisdom. If Isaiah, he may look forward to consolation. If Jeremiah, let him fear punishment.

29. If one sees the Book of Job in a dream, let him fear punishment. One who sees the Scroll of Esther will have a miracle wrought for him.

30. All kinds of beasts are a good sign in a dream, except the elephant, monkey, and the long-tailed ape.

31. All kinds of metal implements are a good sign in a dream, except a hoe, a mattock, and a hatchet.

32. All kinds of fruit are a good sign in a dream, except unripe dates. All kinds of vegetables are a good sign in a dream, except turnip tops.

33. All kinds of colors are a good sign in a dream, except blue.

34. All kinds of birds are a good sign in a dream, except the owl, the horned owl, and the bat.

DREAMS IN MEDIEVAL THOUGHT

Interest in dreams continued through the Middle Ages to modern times, especially among the mystics and the Chassidim. The *Zohar*, the Book of Jewish Mysticism, discusses the problem of the mixing of truth and lies in dreams, and distinguishes between dreams of the wicked and dreams of the righteous. The angel in charge of the dreams of the righteous is Gabriel, and such dreams were considered very close to prophecy itself.

The great medieval philosopher Maimonides, in his *Guide to the Perplexed* (2:36), writes that dreams are a function of a person's imagination only, and not one's intellect. The dream of a prophet, however, is unique in that the prophet's attention must be directed to the knowledge of God. In Maimonides's *Mishneh Torah* (chapter of Fasting 1:12), he avoids the traditional interpretation of the so-called dream fast as a means of protection from impending danger as seen in one's dream. Rather, Maimonides views the purpose of the dream fast as having the educational purpose of self-introspection, whereby a person examines one's deeds and repents of one's mistakes.

Solomon Almoli, a fifteenth-century Spanish philosopher, wrote a work that became popular reading for Eastern European Jews called *Pitron Chalomot* ("Interpretation of Dreams"). In this work he classifies dreams in accordance with their subjects—as animals, plants, angels, the dead, milk, cheese, butter, and so forth. In addition, dreams are rendered with interpretation. For instance, if one dreams that he is gored by an ox, this means that one will have length of years. If one dreams of dreams, this is interpreted to mean that one will earn a great deal of money. Finally, if one dreams of drinking milk, this is interpreted to mean that one will fall ill, but recover rapidly.

OTHER NOTABLE DREAM QUOTATIONS

The following are some interesting quotations from Jewish sources related to dreams and dreaming that will further shed light on the ways in which dreams have been viewed throughout Jewish tradition.

1. Neither a good dream nor a bad dream is wholly fulfilled. (Talmud *Berachot* 55a)

2. The words of dreams neither benefit nor harm. (Talmud *Gittin* 52)

3. A dream that is not interpreted is like a letter that is left unread. (Talmud *Berachot* 55b)

4. Just as wheat cannot be without some straw, so no dream is without some nonsense. (Talmud *Berachot* 55a)

5. If you have a dream which makes you sad, have it interpreted in the presence of three other persons. (Talmud *Berachot* 55b)

6. Dreams lift up fools. (Ben Sirah, Ecclesiasticus, 34:1)

7. A bad dream can be worse than a flogging. (Talmud *Berachot* 55a)

8. A part of a dream may be fulfilled, but never all of it. (Talmud *Berachot* 55a)

9. Three kinds of dreams are fulfilled: a morning dream, a dream that a friend has about one, and a dream that is interpreted in the midst of a dream. Some say: also a dream that is repeated. (Talmud *Berachot* 55b)

10. Rabbi Ze'era said: A person who goes seven days without a dream is called evil. (Talmud *Berachot* 55b)

11. Rabbi Joseph [a blind person] said: In a good dream, the joy is such that, it all but gives me sight. (Talmud *Berachot* 55a)

12. Rabbi Levi said: One should await fulfillment of a good dream for as long as twenty-two years. (Talmud *Berachot* 55b)

13. No dream but has its answer. (Sifre Korach)

14. A man's every act begins with a dream and ends with one. (Theodor Herzl)

FOR FURTHER READING

Birnbaum, P. (1964). *A Book of Jewish Concepts*. New York: Hebrew Publishing Company.

Boteach, S. (1991). *Dreams*. Brooklyn: B.P.

Hausdorff, D. M. (1955). *A Book of Jewish Curiosities*. New York: Bloch Publishing.

Pines, S. transl. (1963). *The Guide of the Perplexed*. Chicago: University of Chicago.

Rosenbaum, B. Z. (1985). *How to Avoid the Evil Eye*. New York: St. Martin's Press.

Sefer Gematriaot, Jewish Theological Seminary Library, New York City.

Trachtenberg, J. (1939). *Jewish Magic and Superstition: A Study in Folk Religion*. New York:Behrman House.

INDEX

ABOUT THE AUTHOR

Rabbi Ronald Isaacs is the rabbi of Temple Sholom in Bridgewater, New Jersey. He received his doctorate in instructional technology from Columbia University's Teacher's College. He is the author of numerous books, including *Jewish Family Matters: A Leaders Guide*, coauthored by Leora Isaacs, *The How to Handbook for Jewish Living*, and *Derech Eretz: Pathway to Ethical Living*. Rabbi Isaacs currently serves on the Board of Shofar Magazine, the Rabbinical Assembly, and C.A.J.E. He resides in New Jersey with his wife, Leora, and their two children Keren and Zachary.